GRAPHIC HISTORY

BETSY ROSS
AND THE AMERICAN FLAG

by Kay Melchisedech Olson
illustrated by Anna Maria Cool,
Sam Delarosa, and Charles Barnett III

Consultant:

Melodie Andrews, PhD

Associate Professor of Early American History

Minnesota State University, Mankato

Capstone
Press

North Mankato, Minnesota

Graphic Library is published by Capstone Press,
1710 Roe Crest Drive, North Mankato, Minnesota 56003.
www.capstonepub.com

Library of Congress Cataloging-in-Publication Data
Olson, Kay Melchisedech.
Betsy Ross and the American flag / by Kay Melchisedech Olson; illustrated by Anna Maria Cool, Sam Delarosa, and Charles Barnett III.
p. cm.—(Graphic library. Graphic history)
Includes bibliographical references and index.
ISBN: 978-0-7368-4962-3 (hardcover)
ISBN: 978-0-7368-6201-1 (softcover pbk.)
1. Ross, Betsy, 1752–1836—Juvenile literature. 2. Revolutionaries—United States—Biography—Juvenile literature. 3. United States—History—Revolution, 1775–1783—Flags—Juvenile literature. 4. Flags—United States—History—18th century—Juvenile literature.
I. Title. II. Series.
E302.6.R77O55 2006
973.3'092—dc22 2005006461

Summary: Describes in graphic format the life of Betsy Ross and the legend of her sewing the first American flag.

Art and Editorial Direction
Jason Knudson and Blake A. Hoena

Designer
Bob Lentz

Colorist
Sarah Trover

Editor
Erika L. Shores

Printed in the United States 5889

TABLE OF CONTENTS

CHAPTER 1
PLAIN AND SIMPLE

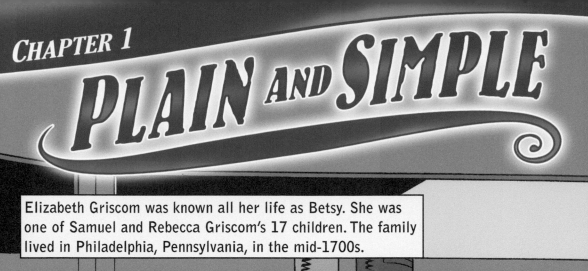

Elizabeth Griscom was known all her life as Betsy. She was one of Samuel and Rebecca Griscom's 17 children. The family lived in Philadelphia, Pennsylvania, in the mid-1700s.

Betsy, hurry and fasten your bonnet. We don't want to be late for Meeting.

Mother, why do we go to Meeting instead of church like my friends?

The Meeting House is the Quaker church.

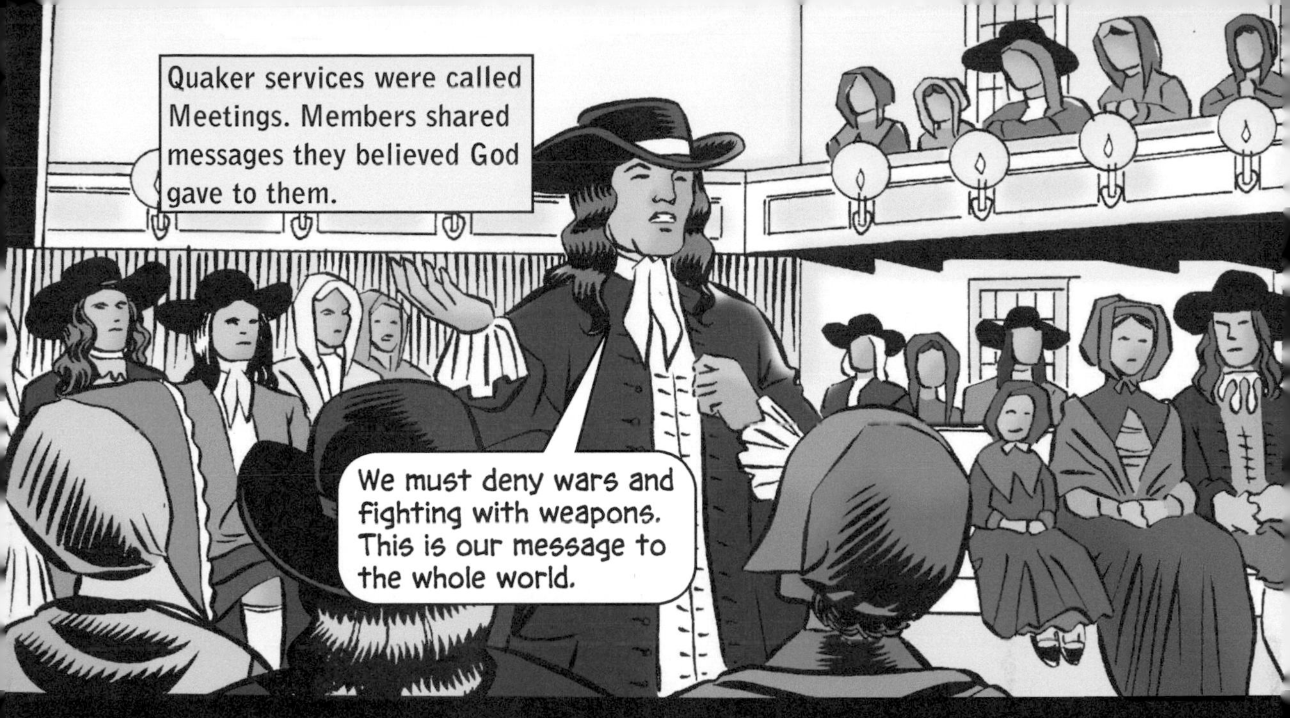
Quaker services were called Meetings. Members shared messages they believed God gave to them.
We must deny wars and fighting with weapons. This is our message to the whole world.

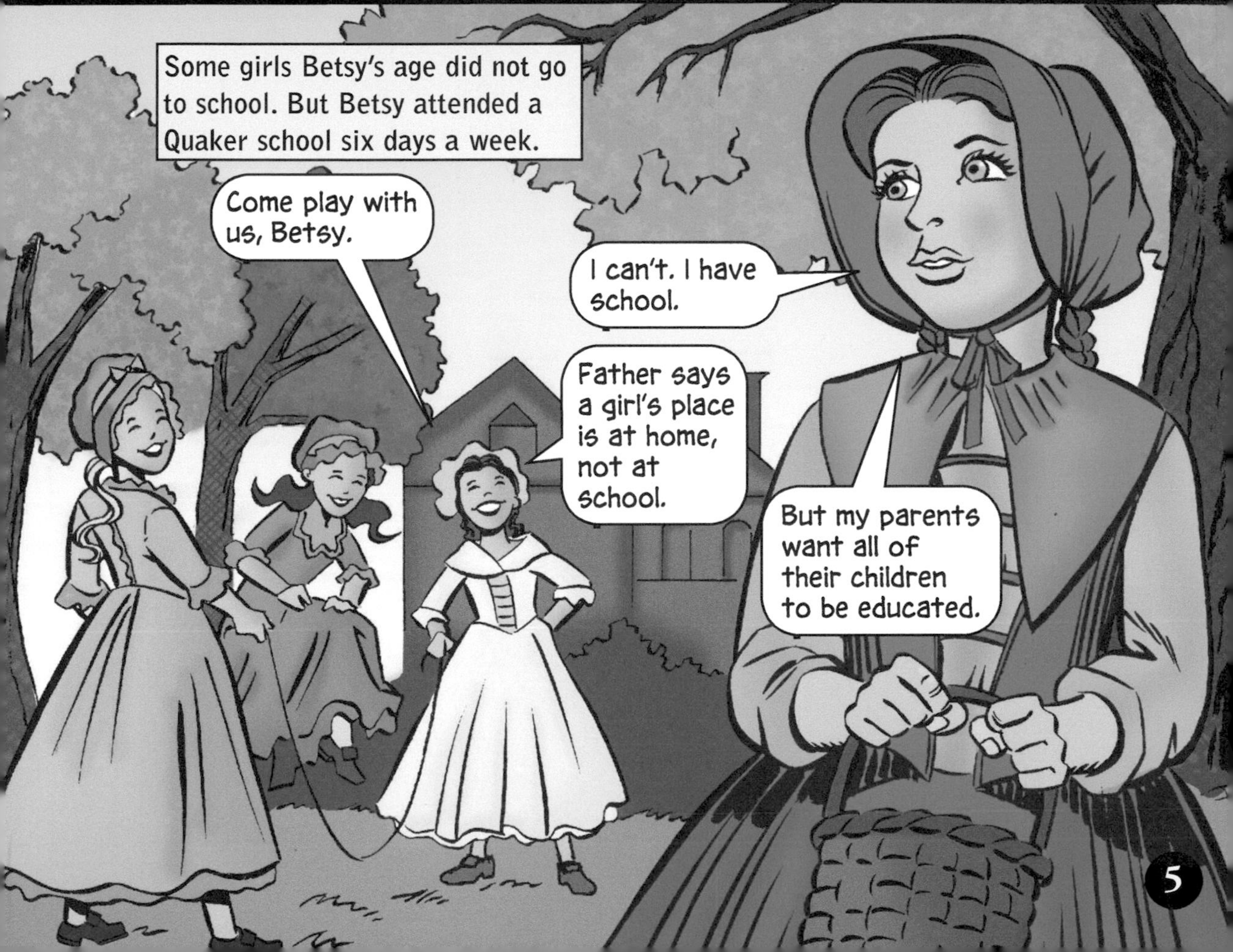
Some girls Betsy's age did not go to school. But Betsy attended a Quaker school six days a week.
Come play with us, Betsy.
I can't. I have school.
Father says a girl's place is at home, not at school.
But my parents want all of their children to be educated.

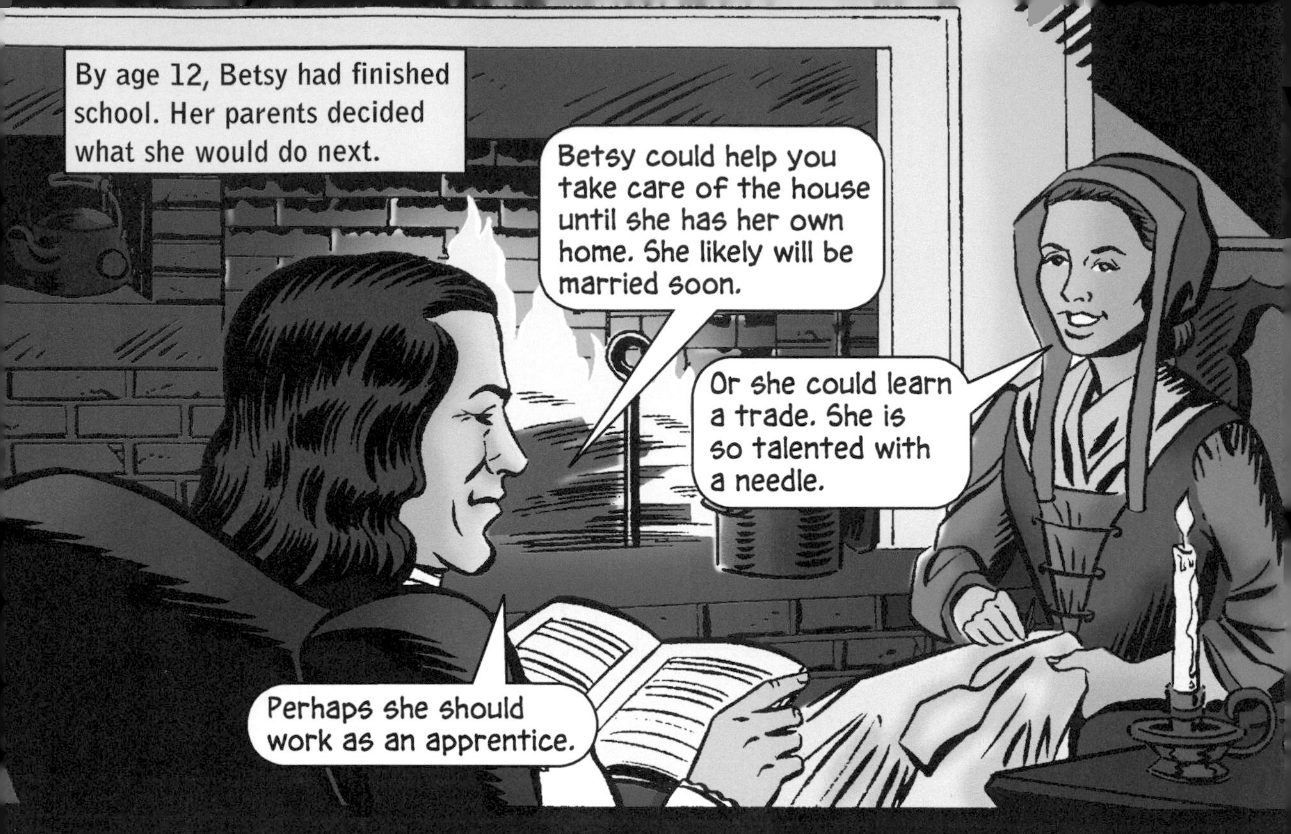
By age 12, Betsy had finished school. Her parents decided what she would do next.
Betsy could help you take care of the house until she has her own home. She likely will be married soon.
Or she could learn a trade. She is so talented with a needle.
Perhaps she should work as an apprentice.

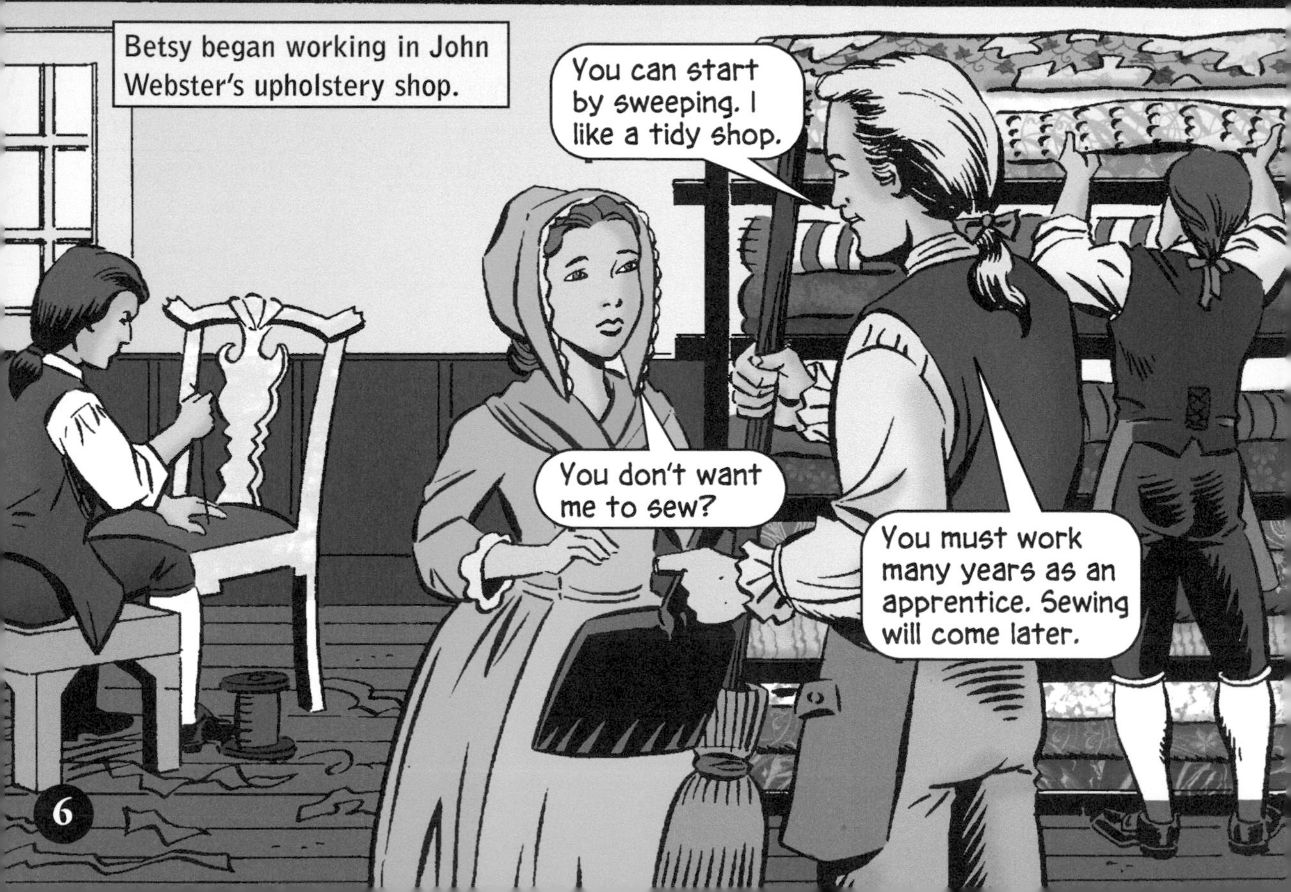
Betsy began working in John Webster's upholstery shop.
You can start by sweeping. I like a tidy shop.
You don't want me to sew?
You must work many years as an apprentice. Sewing will come later.

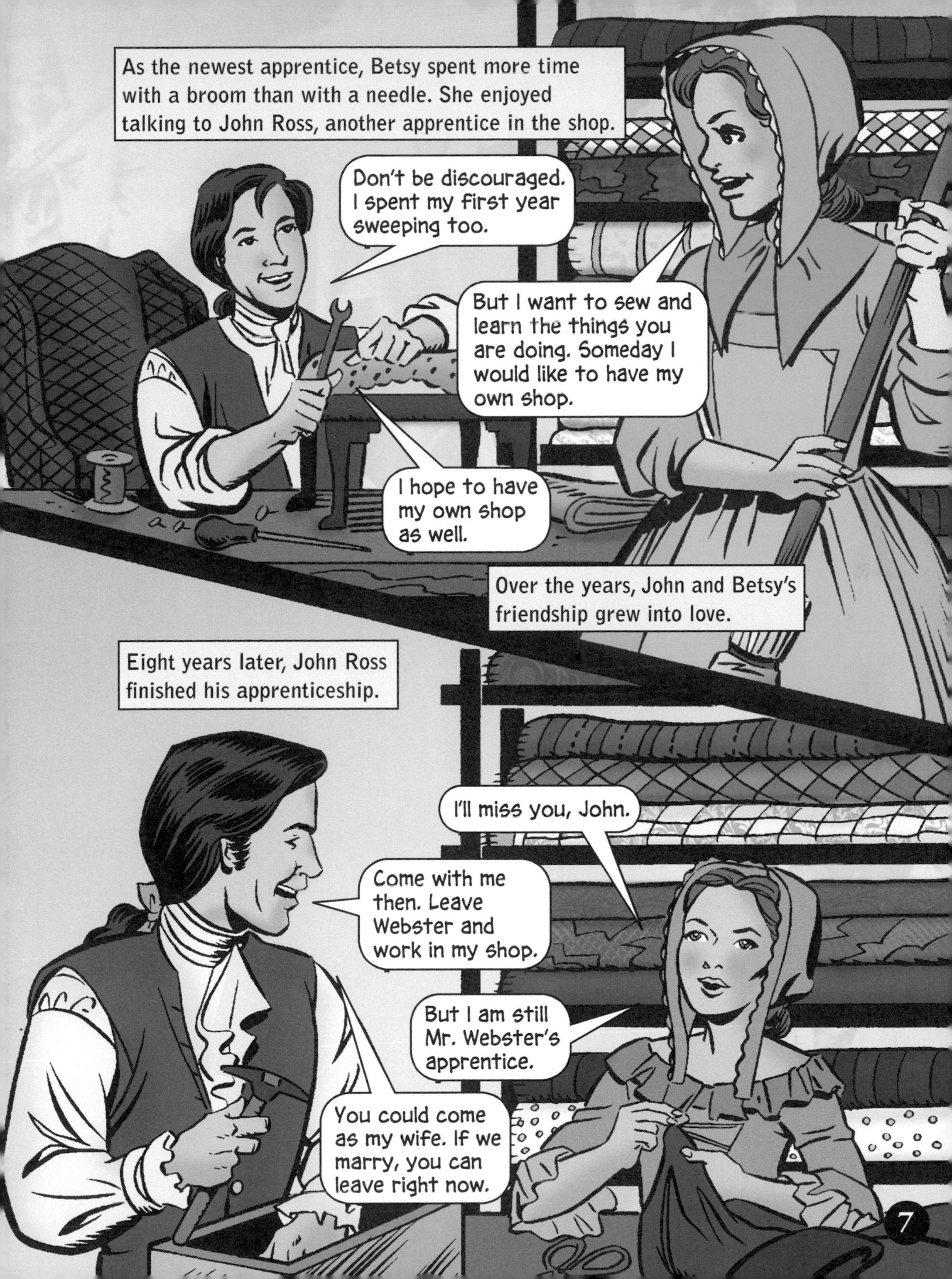
As the newest apprentice, Betsy spent more time with a broom than with a needle. She enjoyed talking to John Ross, another apprentice in the shop.
Don't be discouraged. I spent my first year sweeping too.
But I want to sew and learn the things you are doing. Someday I would like to have my own shop.
I hope to have my own shop as well.
Over the years, John and Betsy's friendship grew into love.
Eight years later, John Ross finished his apprenticeship.
I'll miss you, John.
Come with me then. Leave Webster and work in my shop.
But I am still Mr. Webster's apprentice.
You could come as my wife. If we marry, you can leave right now.

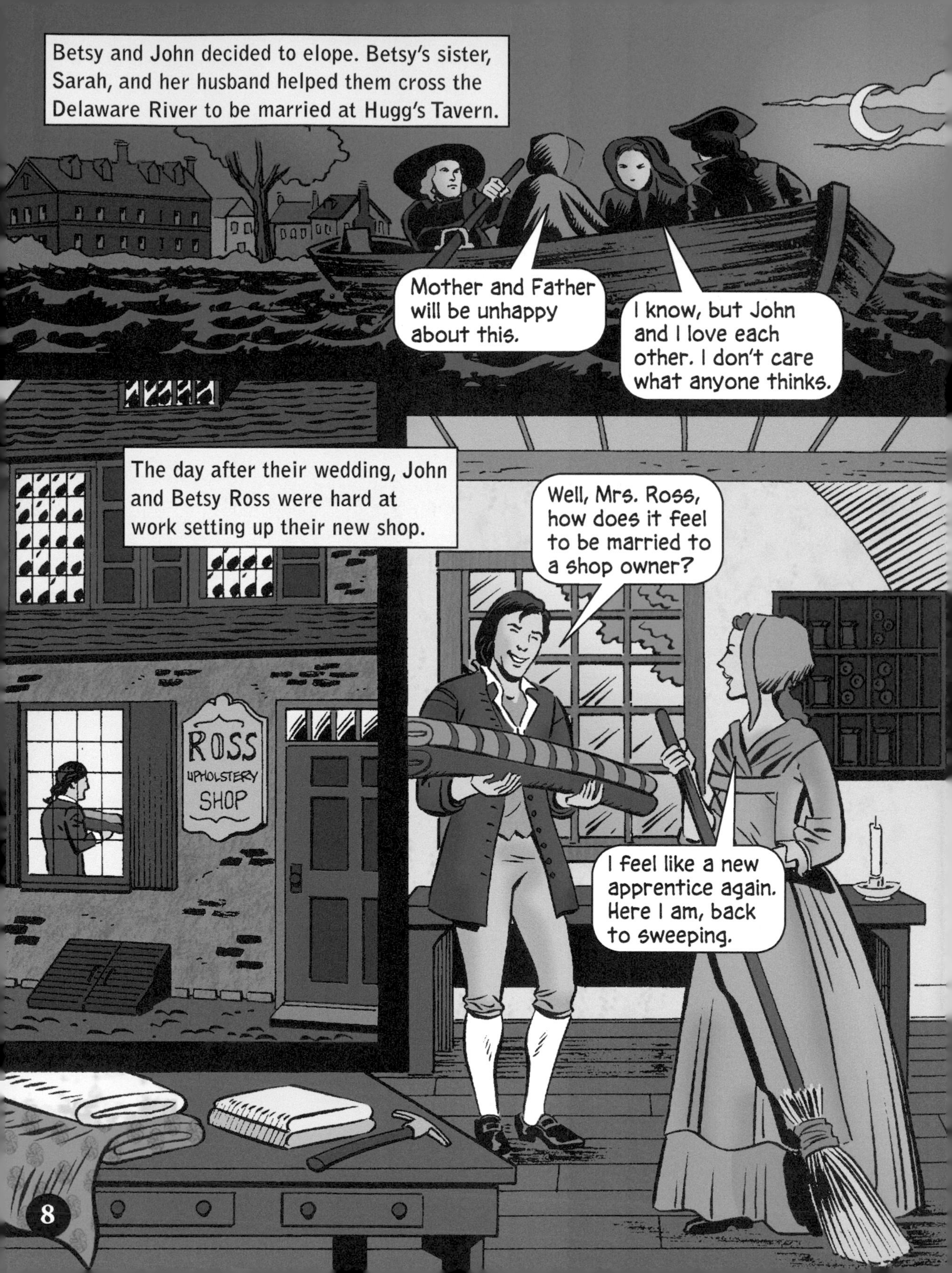
Betsy and John decided to elope. Betsy's sister, Sarah, and her husband helped them cross the Delaware River to be married at Hugg's Tavern.
Mother and Father will be unhappy about this.
I know, but John and I love each other. I don't care what anyone thinks.
The day after their wedding, John and Betsy Ross were hard at work setting up their new shop.
ROSS UPHOLSTERY SHOP
Well, Mrs. Ross, how does it feel to be married to a shop owner?
I feel like a new apprentice again. Here I am, back to sweeping.

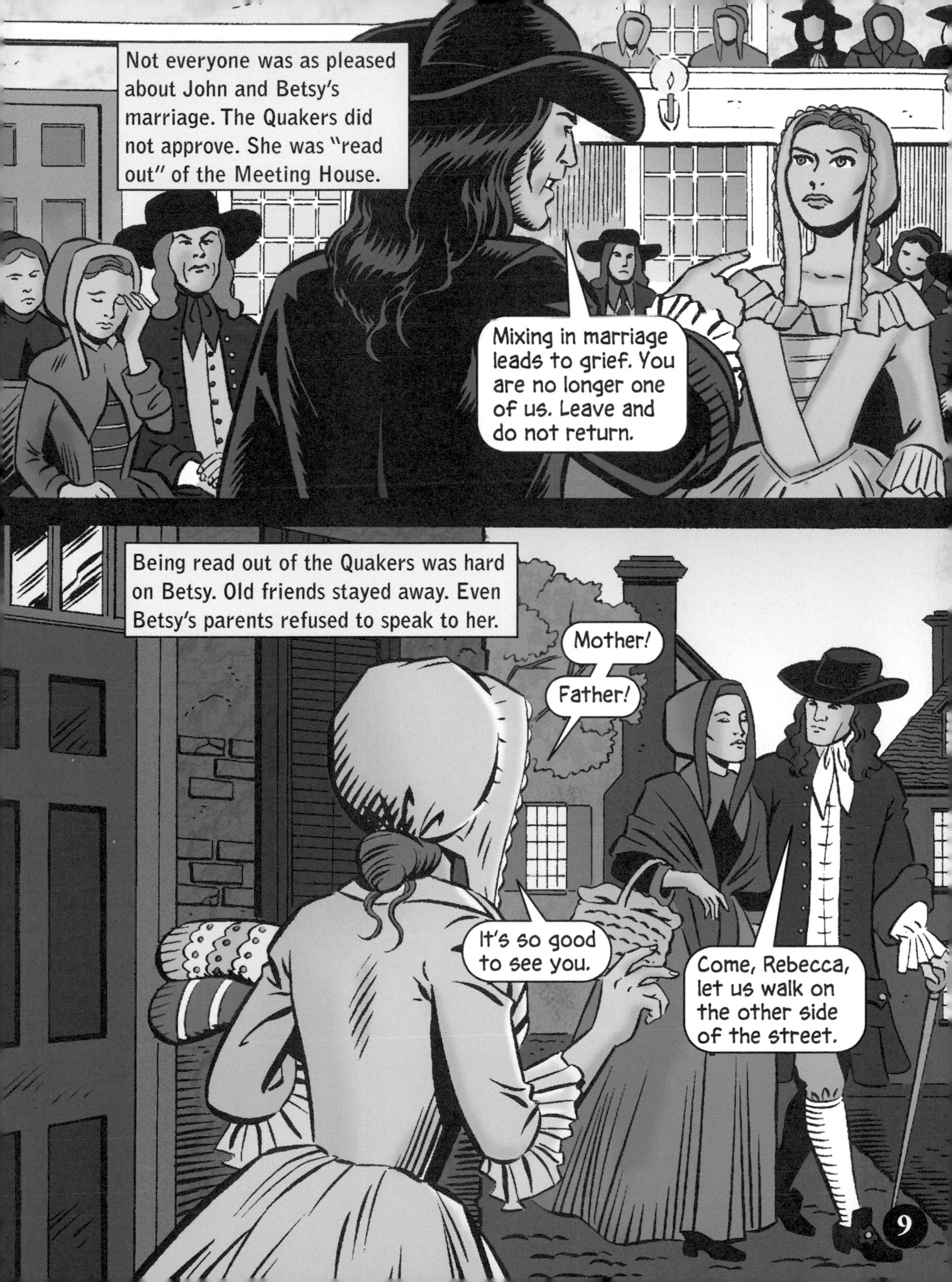
Not everyone was as pleased about John and Betsy's marriage. The Quakers did not approve. She was "read out" of the Meeting House.
Mixing in marriage leads to grief. You are no longer one of us. Leave and do not return.
Being read out of the Quakers was hard on Betsy. Old friends stayed away. Even Betsy's parents refused to speak to her.
Mother!
Father!
It's so good to see you.
Come, Rebecca, let us walk on the other side of the street.

Chapter 2
Troubled Times

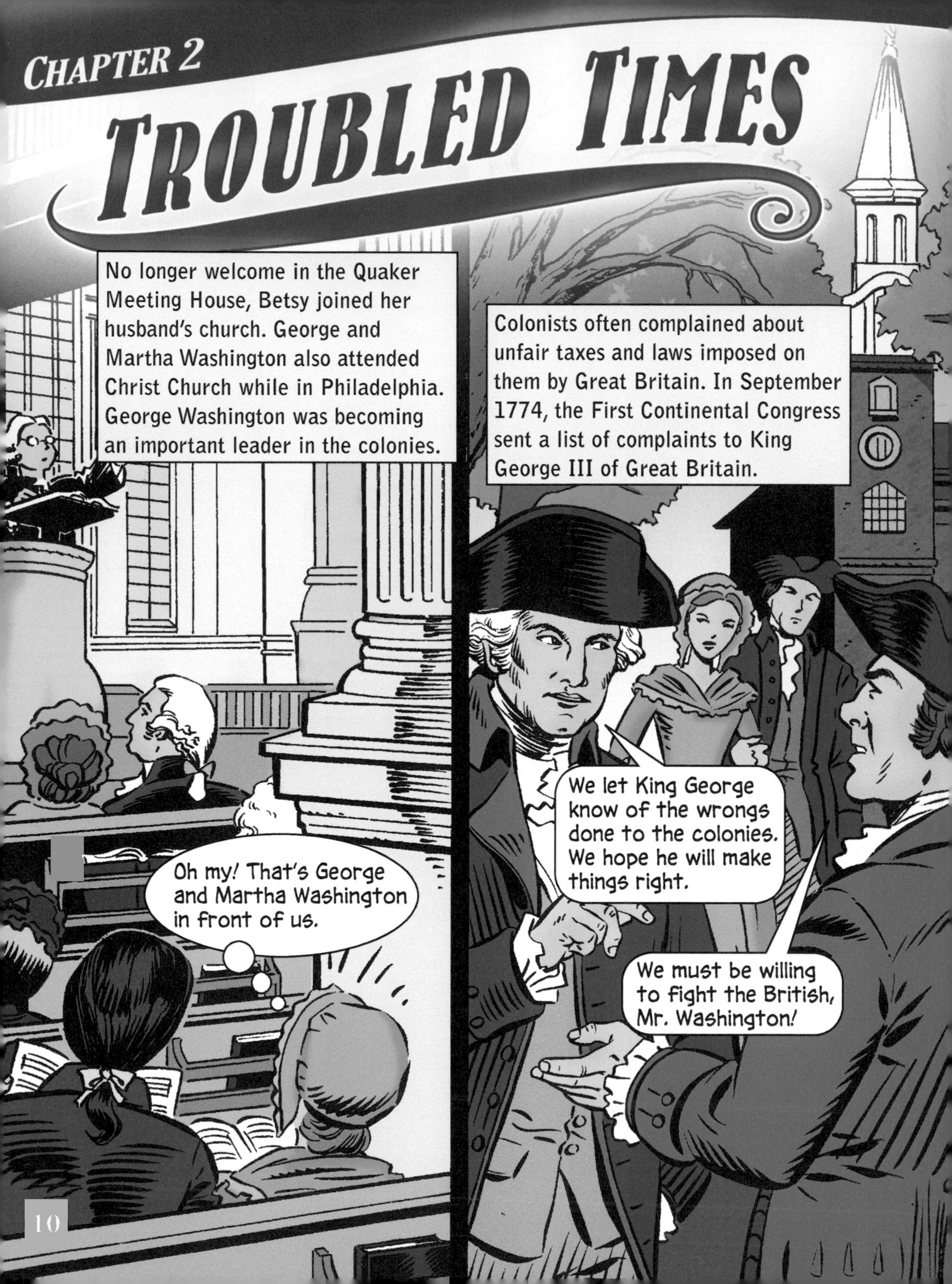
No longer welcome in the Quaker Meeting House, Betsy joined her husband's church. George and Martha Washington also attended Christ Church while in Philadelphia. George Washington was becoming an important leader in the colonies.
Oh my! That's George and Martha Washington in front of us.
Colonists often complained about unfair taxes and laws imposed on them by Great Britain. In September 1774, the First Continental Congress sent a list of complaints to King George III of Great Britain.
We let King George know of the wrongs done to the colonies. We hope he will make things right.
We must be willing to fight the British, Mr. Washington!

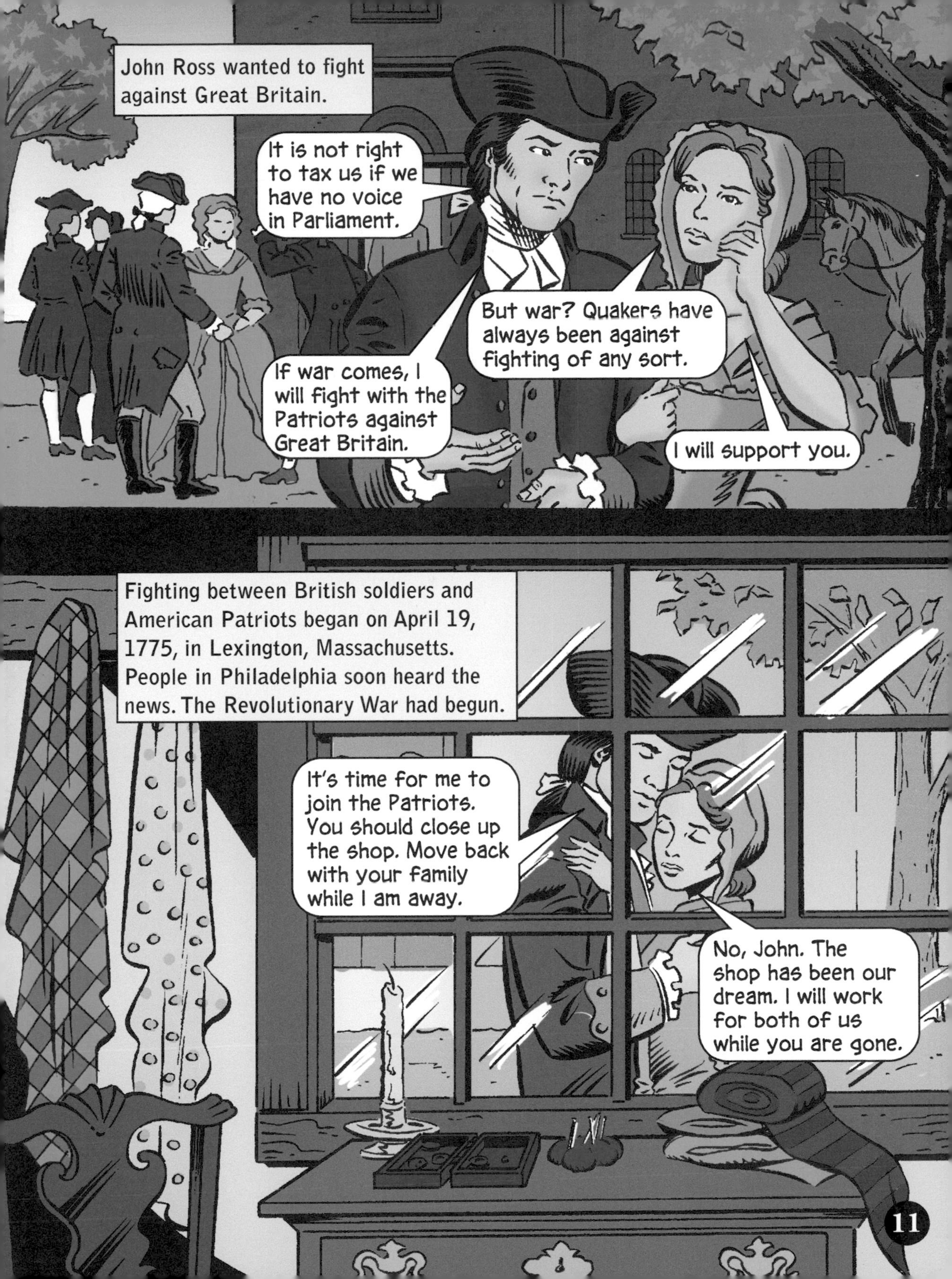
John Ross wanted to fight against Great Britain.
It is not right to tax us if we have no voice in Parliament.
But war? Quakers have always been against fighting of any sort.
If war comes, I will fight with the Patriots against Great Britain.
I will support you.
Fighting between British soldiers and American Patriots began on April 19, 1775, in Lexington, Massachusetts. People in Philadelphia soon heard the news. The Revolutionary War had begun.
It's time for me to join the Patriots. You should close up the shop. Move back with your family while I am away.
No, John. The shop has been our dream. I will work for both of us while you are gone.

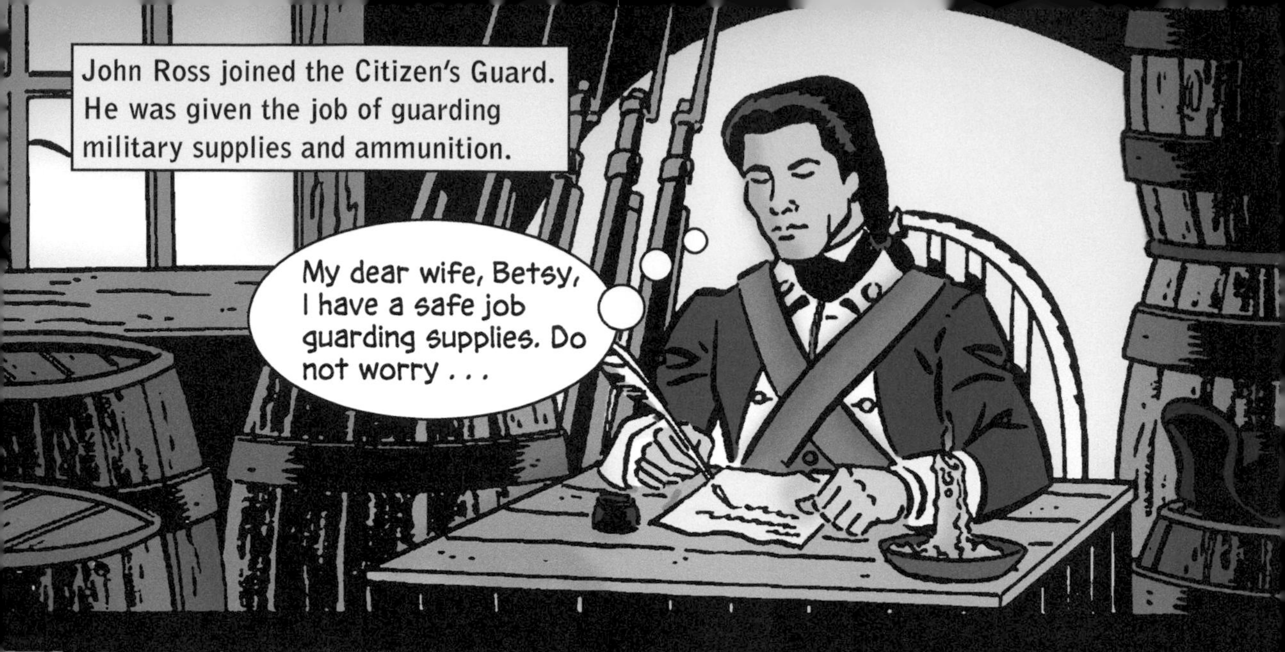
John Ross joined the Citizen's Guard. He was given the job of guarding military supplies and ammunition.
My dear wife, Betsy, I have a safe job guarding supplies. Do not worry . . .

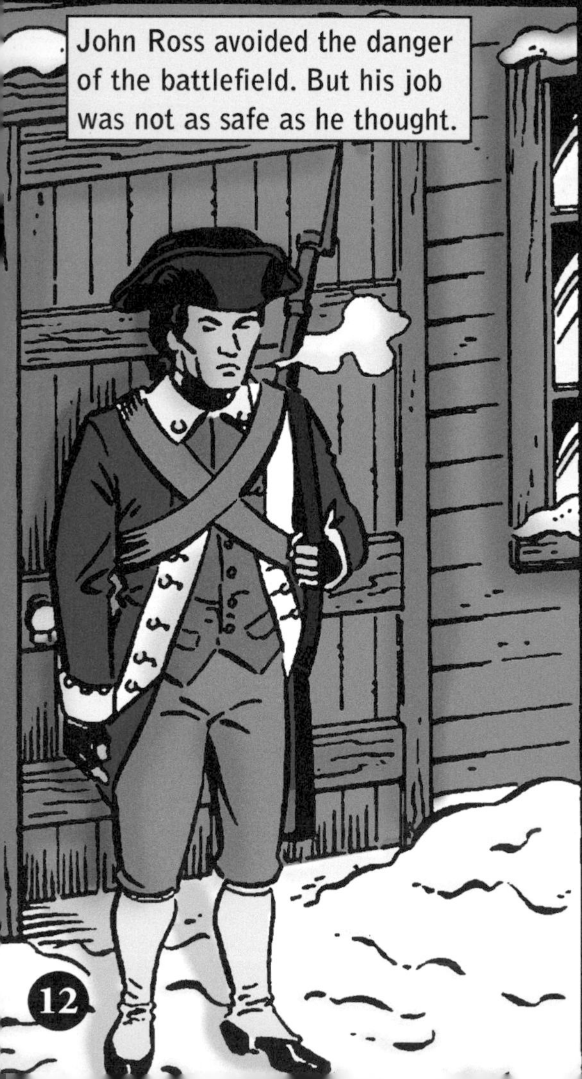
John Ross avoided the danger of the battlefield. But his job was not as safe as he thought.

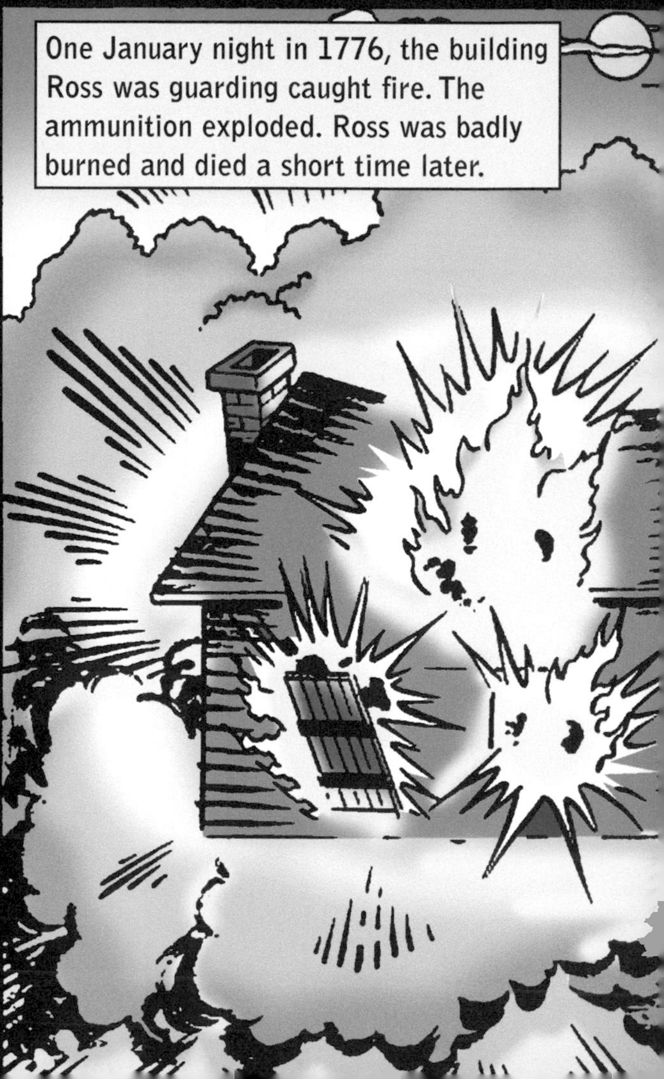
One January night in 1776, the building Ross was guarding caught fire. The ammunition exploded. Ross was badly burned and died a short time later.

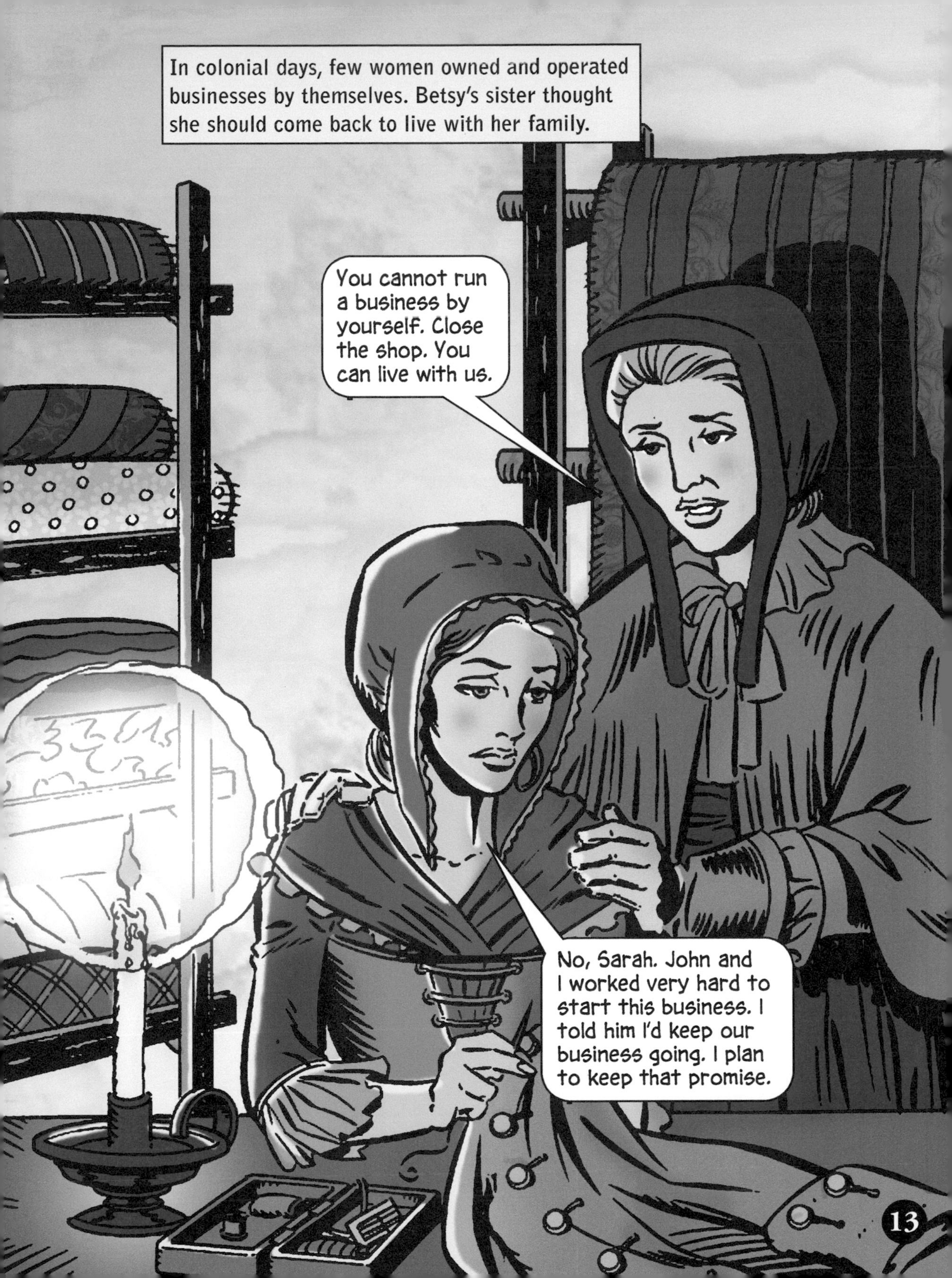
In colonial days, few women owned and operated businesses by themselves. Betsy's sister thought she should come back to live with her family.
You cannot run a business by yourself. Close the shop. You can live with us.
No, Sarah. John and I worked very hard to start this business. I told him I'd keep our business going. I plan to keep that promise.

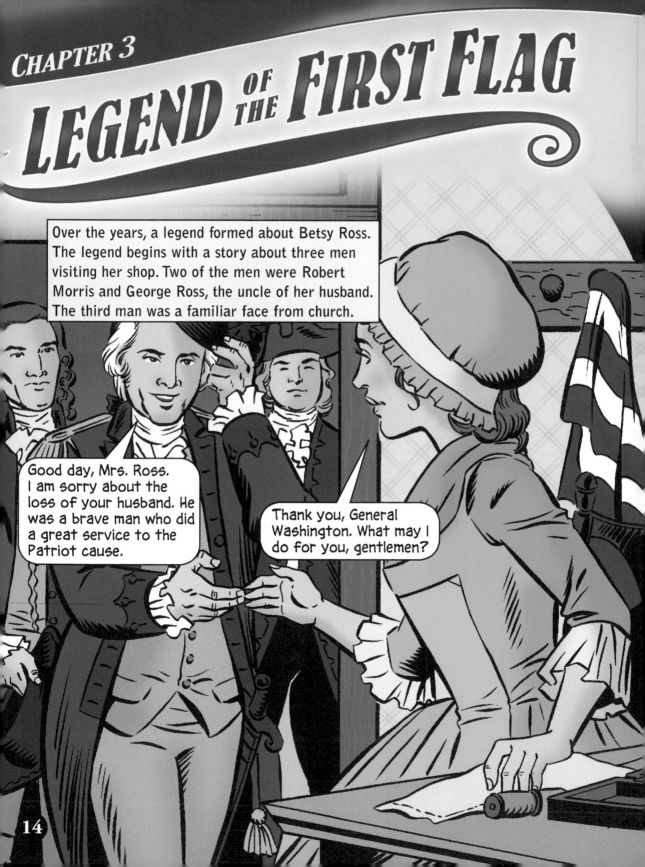

CHAPTER 3
LEGEND OF THE FIRST FLAG

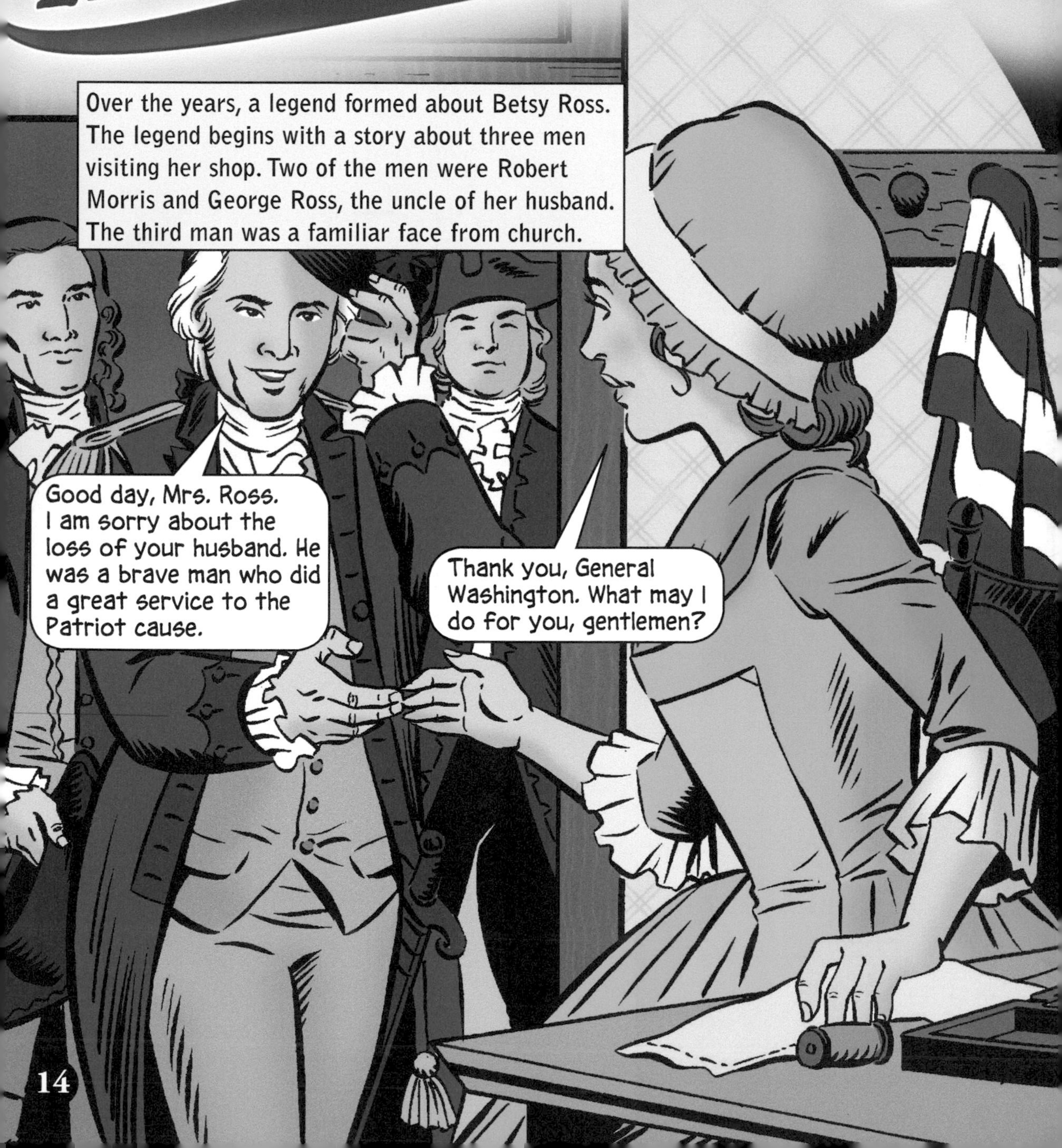

Over the years, a legend formed about Betsy Ross. The legend begins with a story about three men visiting her shop. Two of the men were Robert Morris and George Ross, the uncle of her husband. The third man was a familiar face from church.
Good day, Mrs. Ross. I am sorry about the loss of your husband. He was a brave man who did a great service to the Patriot cause.
Thank you, General Washington. What may I do for you, gentlemen?

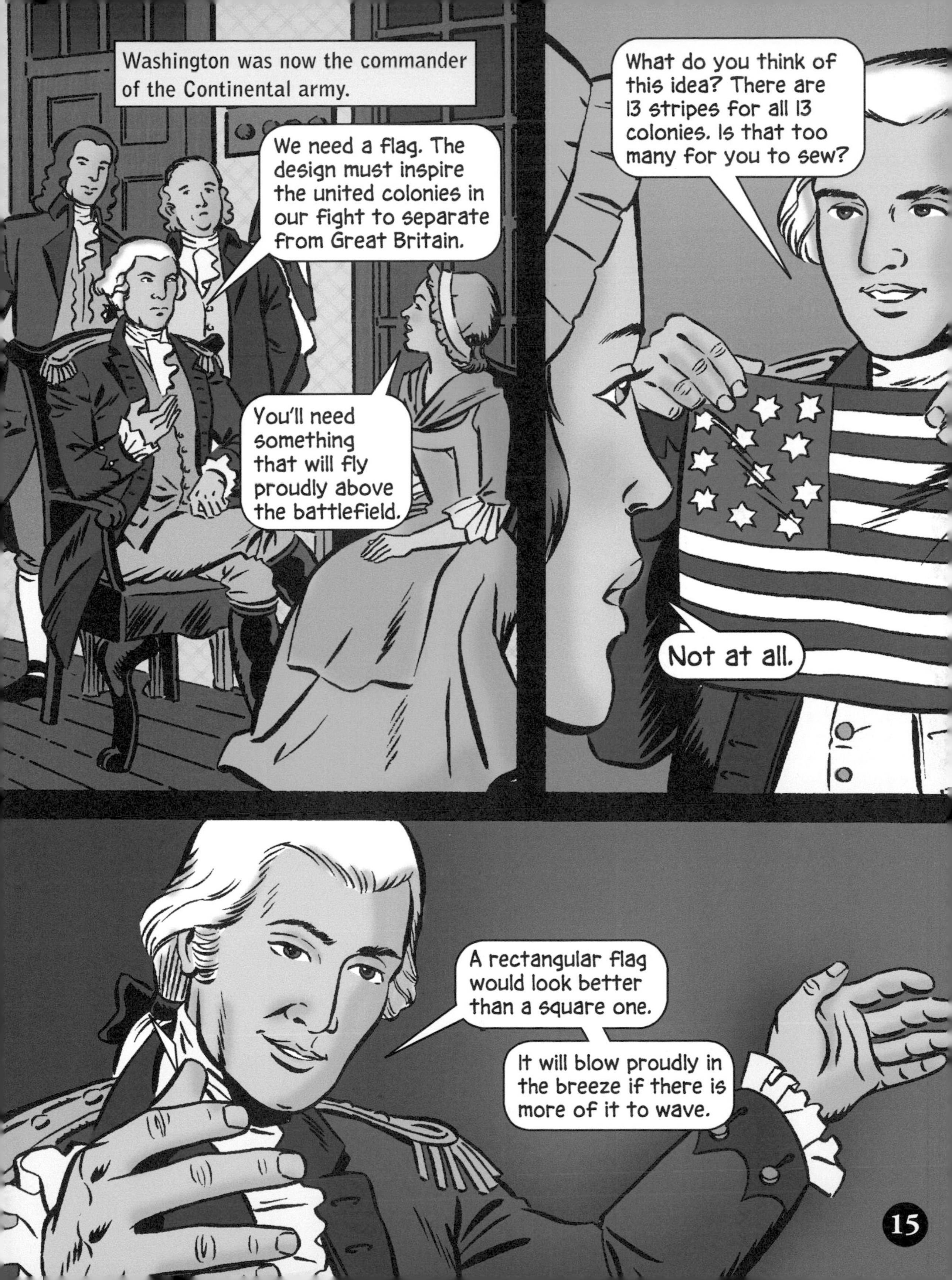
Washington was now the commander of the Continental army.
We need a flag. The design must inspire the united colonies in our fight to separate from Great Britain.
You'll need something that will fly proudly above the battlefield.
What do you think of this idea? There are 13 stripes for all 13 colonies. Is that too many for you to sew?
Not at all.
A rectangular flag would look better than a square one.
It will blow proudly in the breeze if there is more of it to wave.

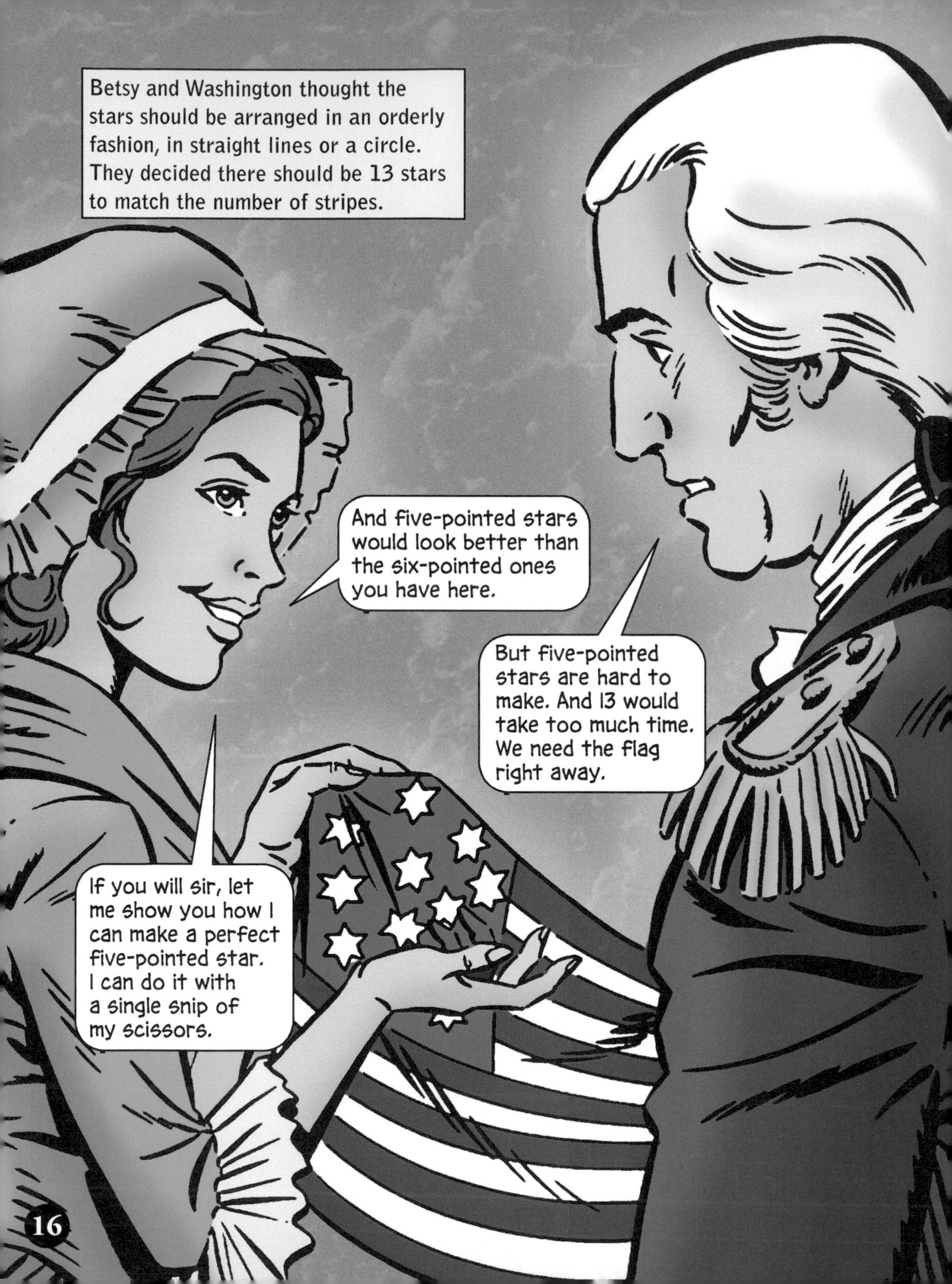

Betsy and Washington thought the stars should be arranged in an orderly fashion, in straight lines or a circle. They decided there should be 13 stars to match the number of stripes.
And five-pointed stars would look better than the six-pointed ones you have here.
But five-pointed stars are hard to make. And 13 would take too much time. We need the flag right away.
If you will sir, let me show you how I can make a perfect five-pointed star. I can do it with a single snip of my scissors.

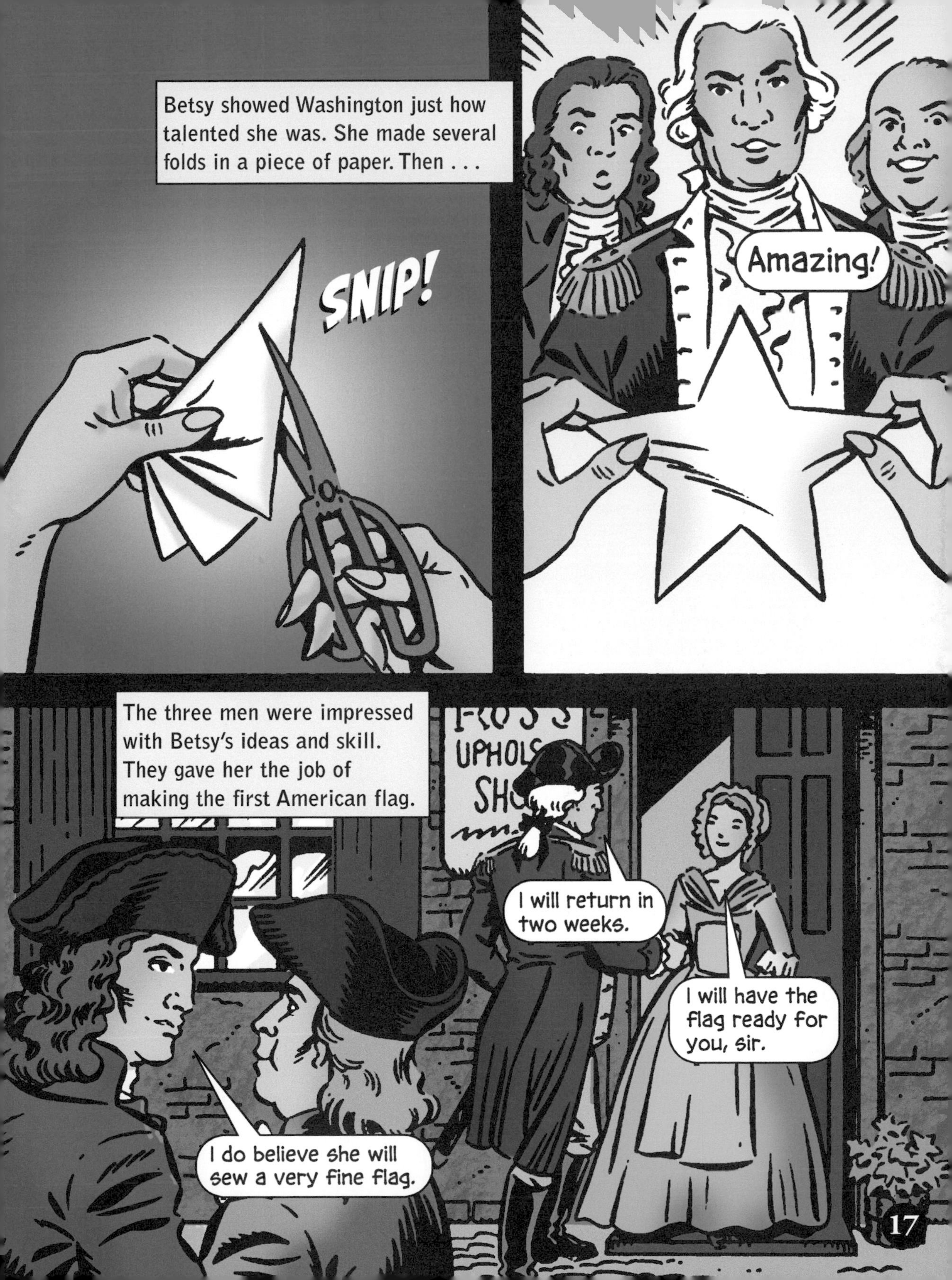
Betsy showed Washington just how talented she was. She made several folds in a piece of paper. Then . . .
SNIP!
Amazing!
The three men were impressed with Betsy's ideas and skill. They gave her the job of making the first American flag.
I will return in two weeks.
I will have the flag ready for you, sir.
I do believe she will sew a very fine flag.

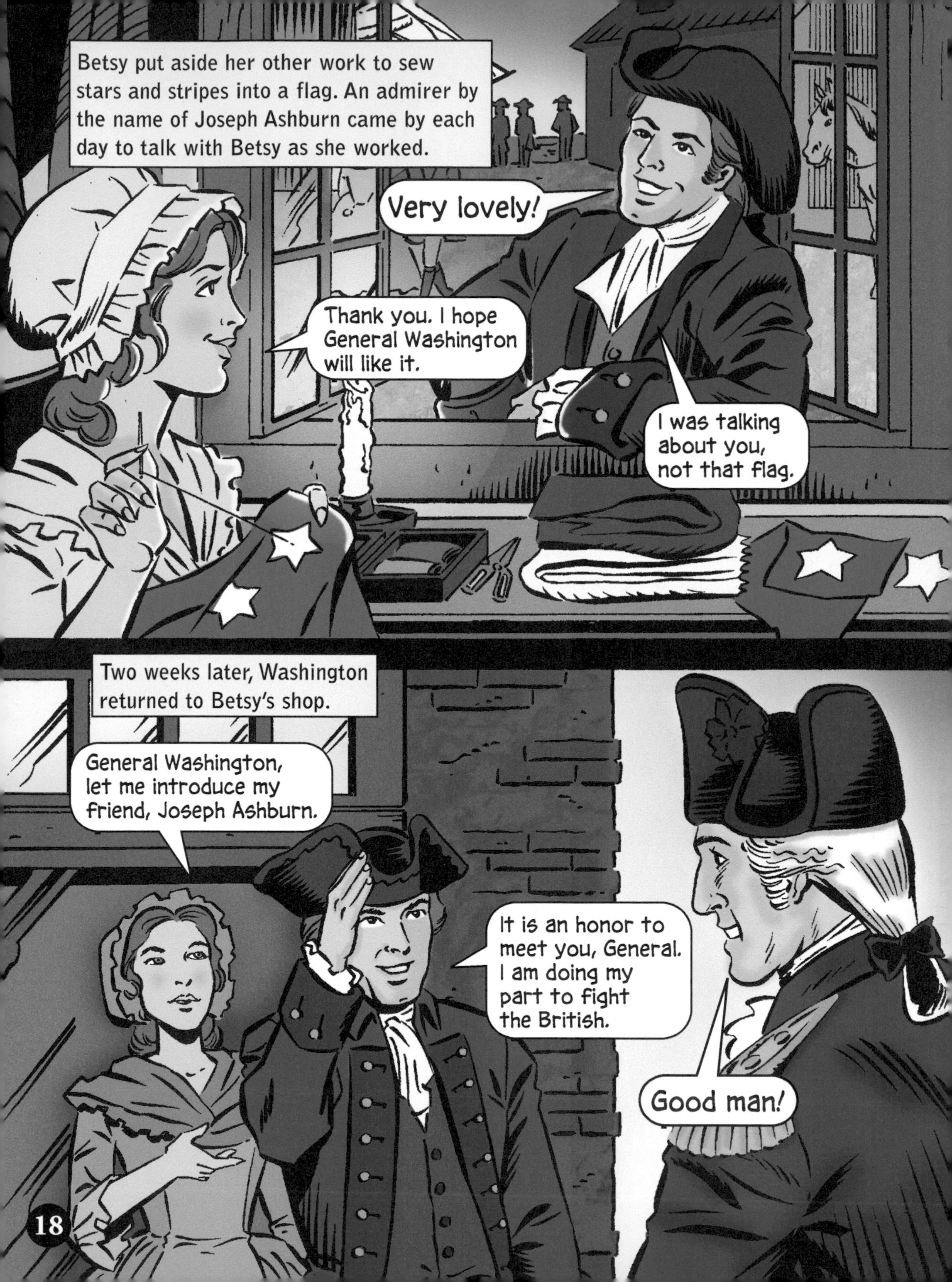
Betsy put aside her other work to sew stars and stripes into a flag. An admirer by the name of Joseph Ashburn came by each day to talk with Betsy as she worked.
Very lovely!
Thank you. I hope General Washington will like it.
I was talking about you, not that flag.
Two weeks later, Washington returned to Betsy's shop.
General Washington, let me introduce my friend, Joseph Ashburn.
It is an honor to meet you, General. I am doing my part to fight the British.
Good man!

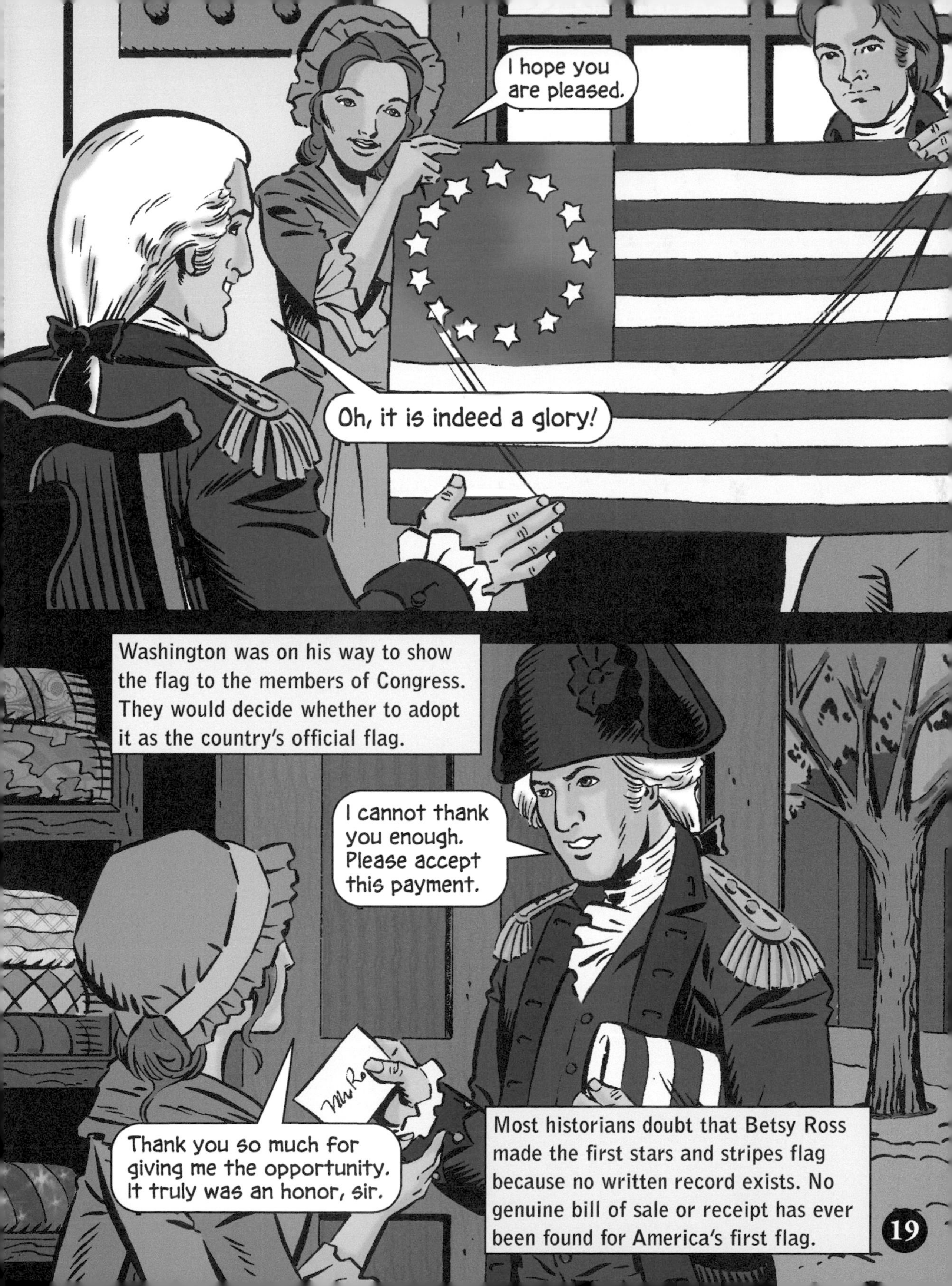
I hope you are pleased.
Oh, it is indeed a glory!
Washington was on his way to show the flag to the members of Congress. They would decide whether to adopt it as the country's official flag.
I cannot thank you enough. Please accept this payment.
Thank you so much for giving me the opportunity. It truly was an honor, sir.
Most historians doubt that Betsy Ross made the first stars and stripes flag because no written record exists. No genuine bill of sale or receipt has ever been found for America's first flag.

Chapter 4

The Story Goes On

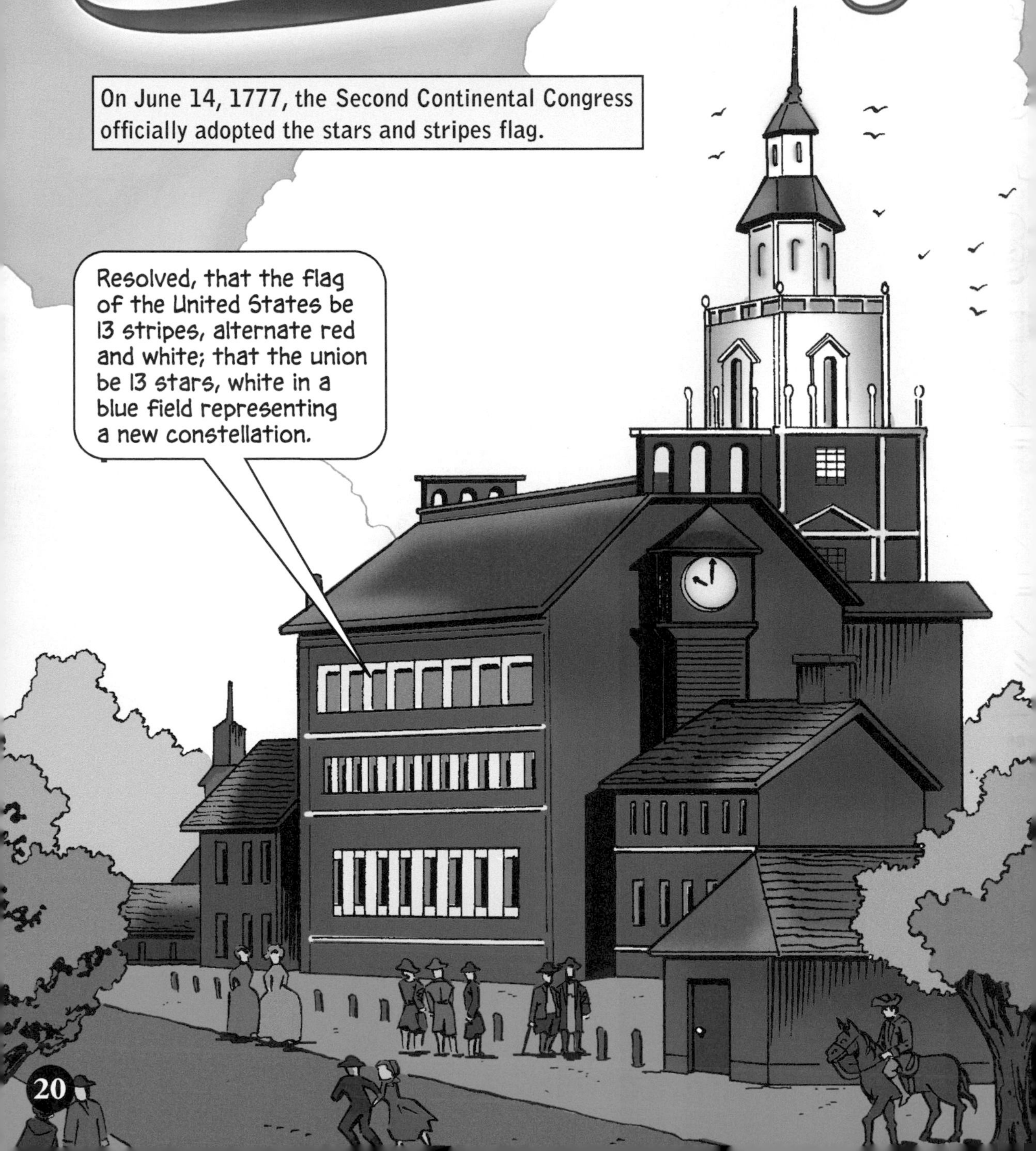

On June 14, 1777, the Second Continental Congress officially adopted the stars and stripes flag.
Resolved, that the flag of the United States be 13 stripes, alternate red and white; that the union be 13 stars, white in a blue field representing a new constellation.

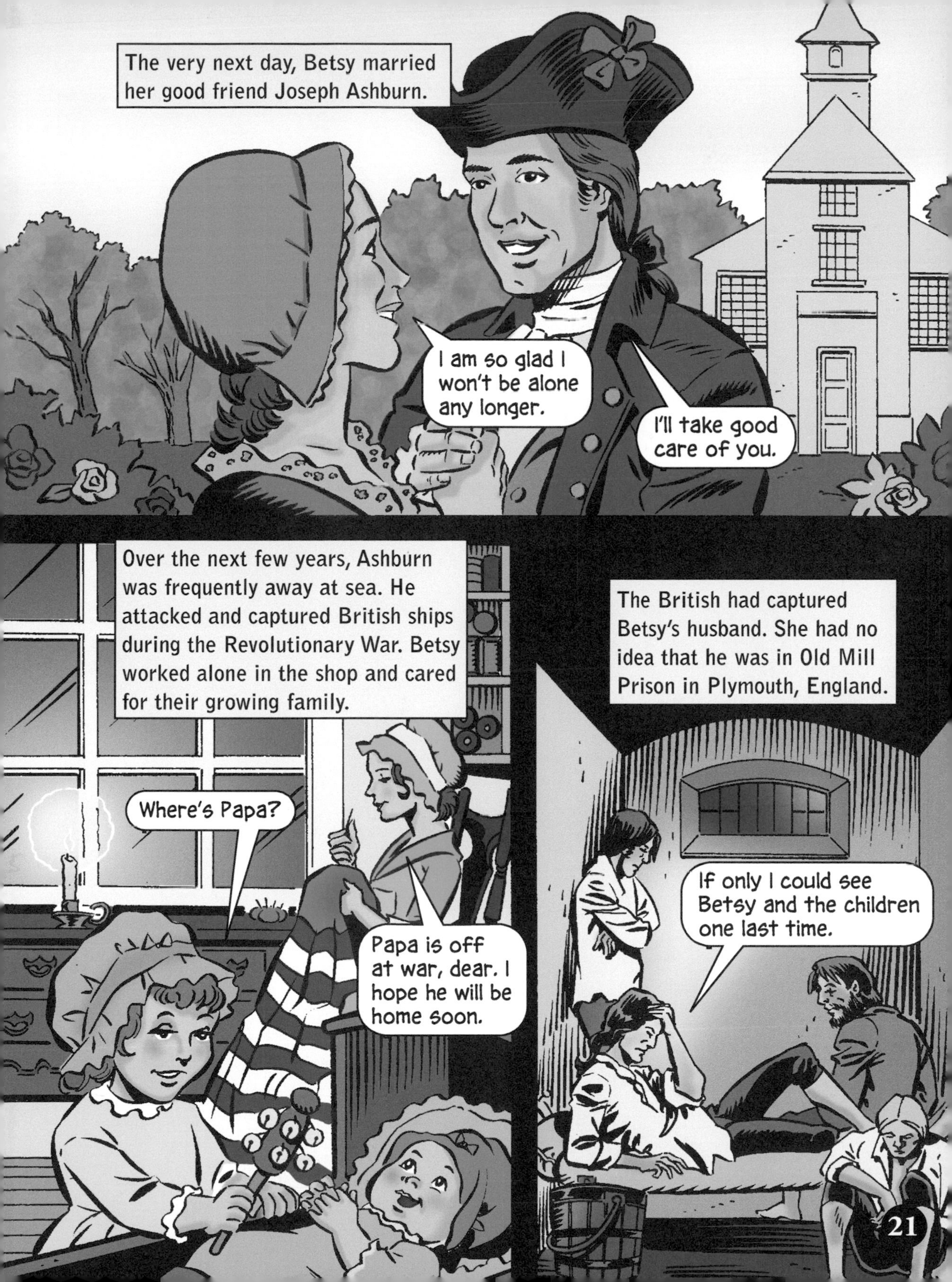
The very next day, Betsy married her good friend Joseph Ashburn.
I am so glad I won't be alone any longer.
I'll take good care of you.
Over the next few years, Ashburn was frequently away at sea. He attacked and captured British ships during the Revolutionary War. Betsy worked alone in the shop and cared for their growing family.
Where's Papa?
Papa is off at war, dear. I hope he will be home soon.
The British had captured Betsy's husband. She had no idea that he was in Old Mill Prison in Plymouth, England.
If only I could see Betsy and the children one last time.

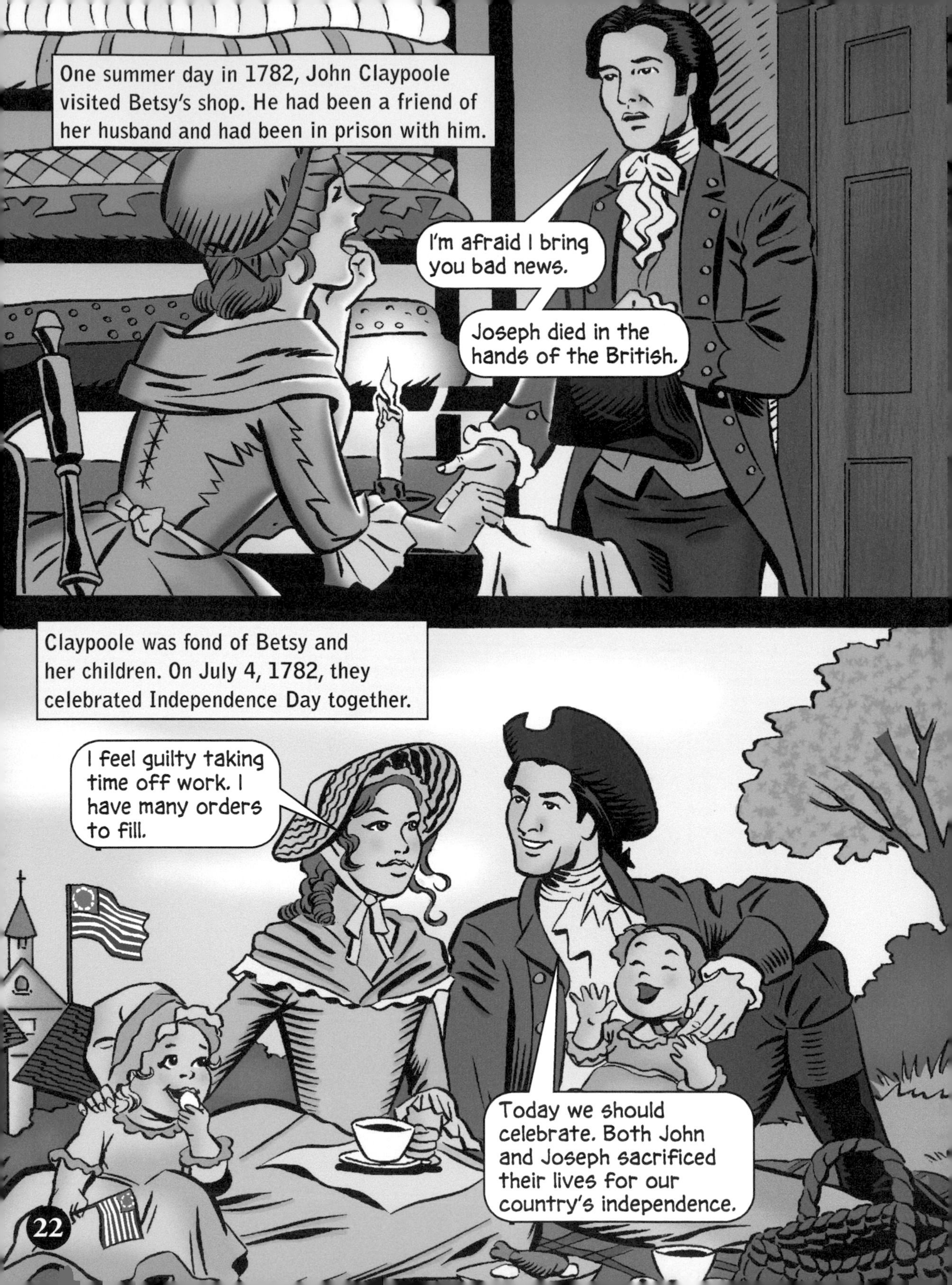
One summer day in 1782, John Claypoole visited Betsy's shop. He had been a friend of her husband and had been in prison with him.
I'm afraid I bring you bad news.
Joseph died in the hands of the British.
Claypoole was fond of Betsy and her children. On July 4, 1782, they celebrated Independence Day together.
I feel guilty taking time off work. I have many orders to fill.
Today we should celebrate. Both John and Joseph sacrificed their lives for our country's independence.

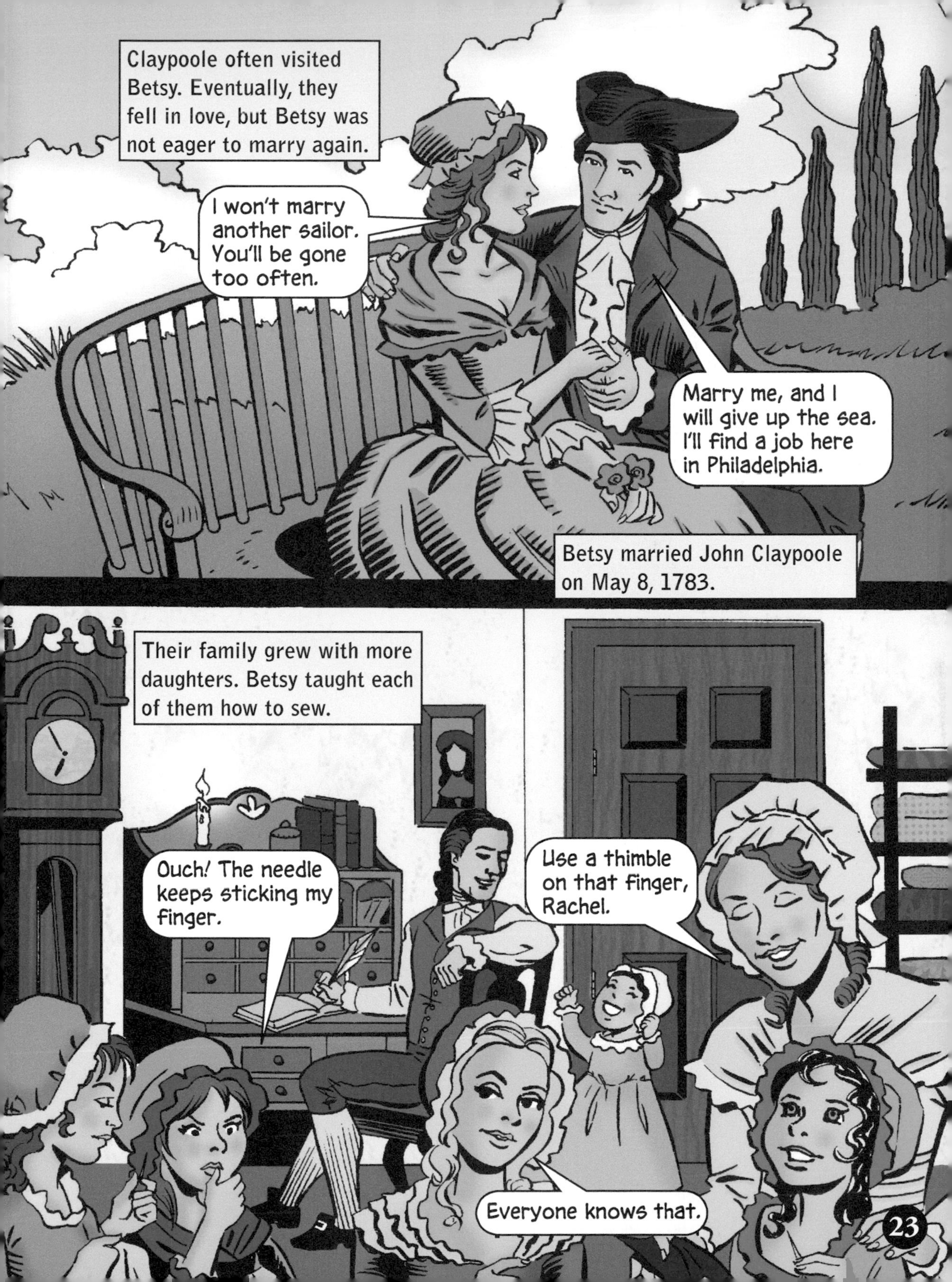
Claypoole often visited Betsy. Eventually, they fell in love, but Betsy was not eager to marry again.
I won't marry another sailor. You'll be gone too often.
Marry me, and I will give up the sea. I'll find a job here in Philadelphia.
Betsy married John Claypoole on May 8, 1783.
Their family grew with more daughters. Betsy taught each of them how to sew.
Ouch! The needle keeps sticking my finger.
Use a thimble on that finger, Rachel.
Everyone knows that.

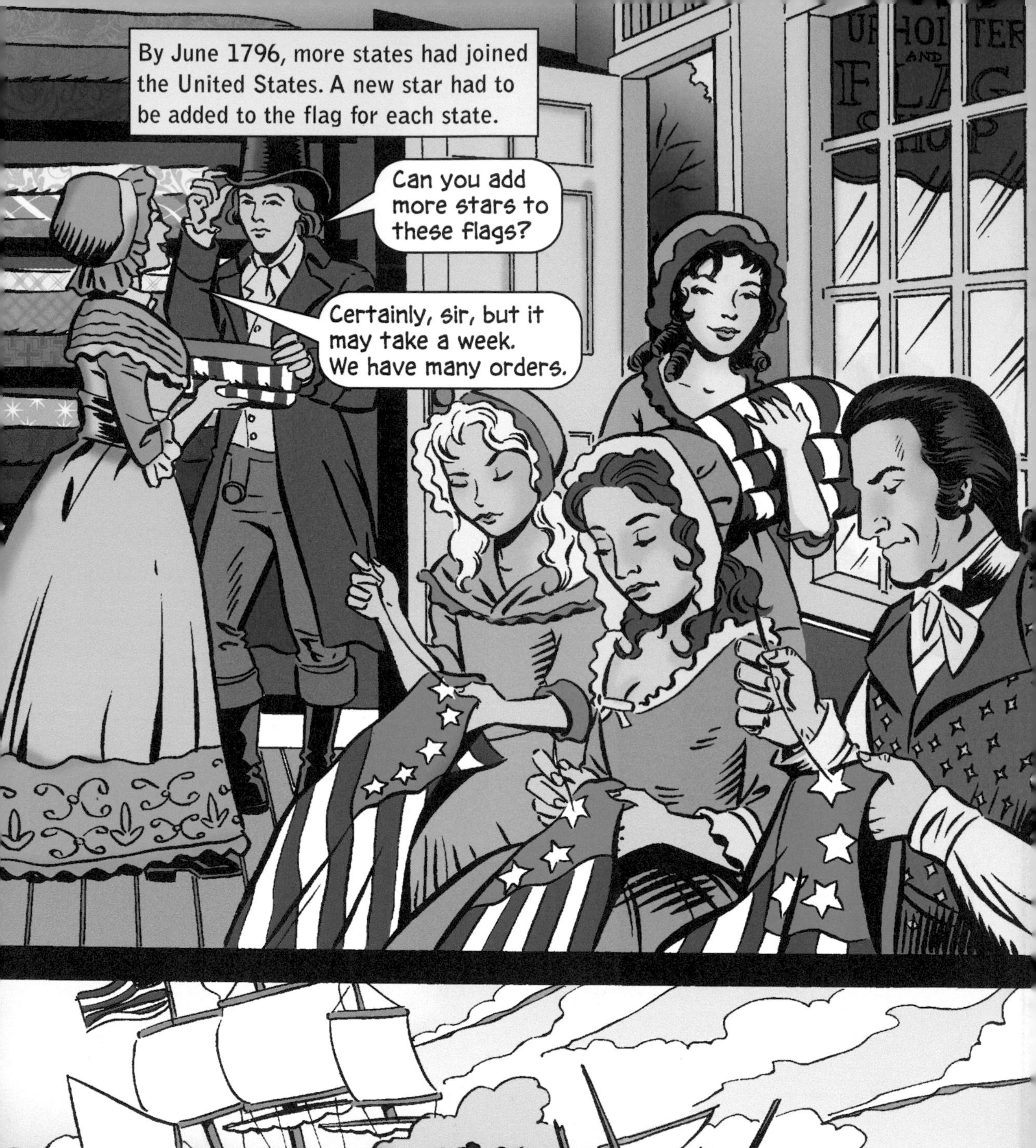
By June 1796, more states had joined the United States. A new star had to be added to the flag for each state.
Can you add more stars to these flags?
Certainly, sir, but it may take a week. We have many orders.

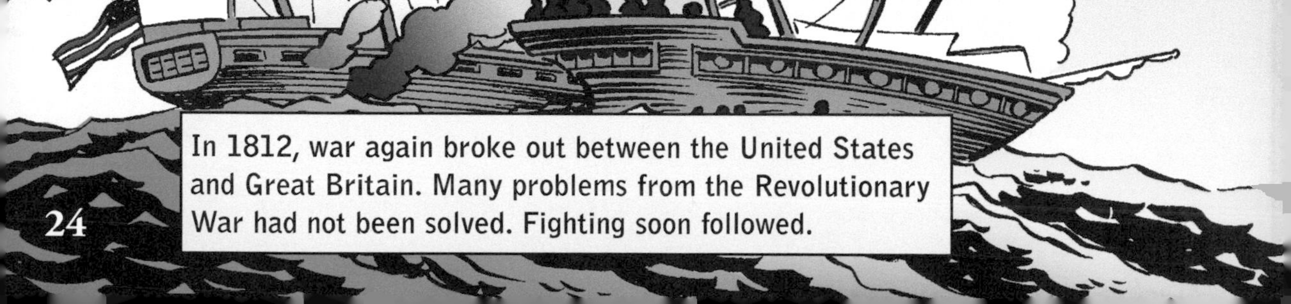
In 1812, war again broke out between the United States and Great Britain. Many problems from the Revolutionary War had not been solved. Fighting soon followed.

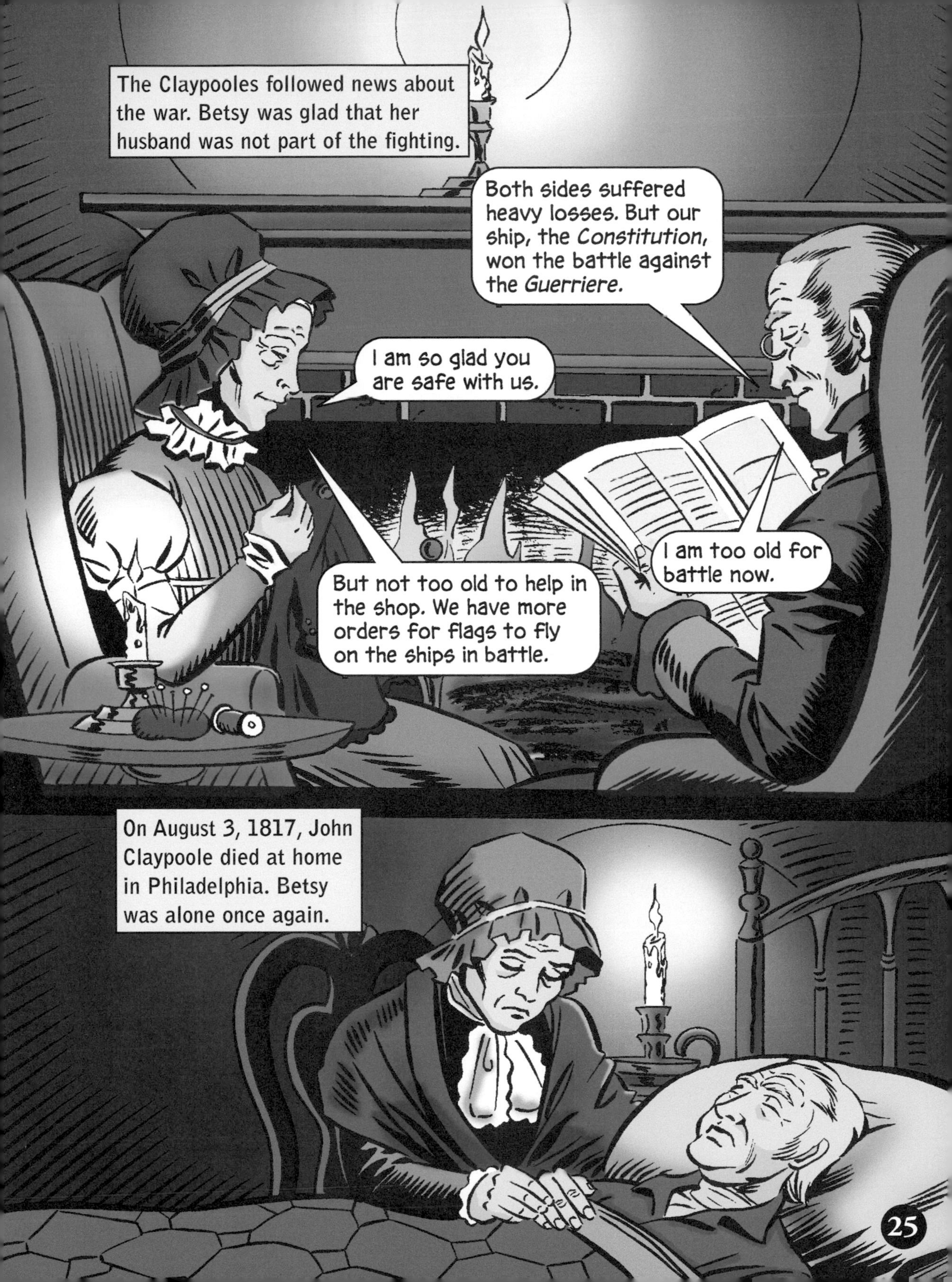
The Claypooles followed news about the war. Betsy was glad that her husband was not part of the fighting.
Both sides suffered heavy losses. But our ship, the *Constitution*, won the battle against the *Guerriere*.
I am so glad you are safe with us.
I am too old for battle now.
But not too old to help in the shop. We have more orders for flags to fly on the ships in battle.
On August 3, 1817, John Claypoole died at home in Philadelphia. Betsy was alone once again.

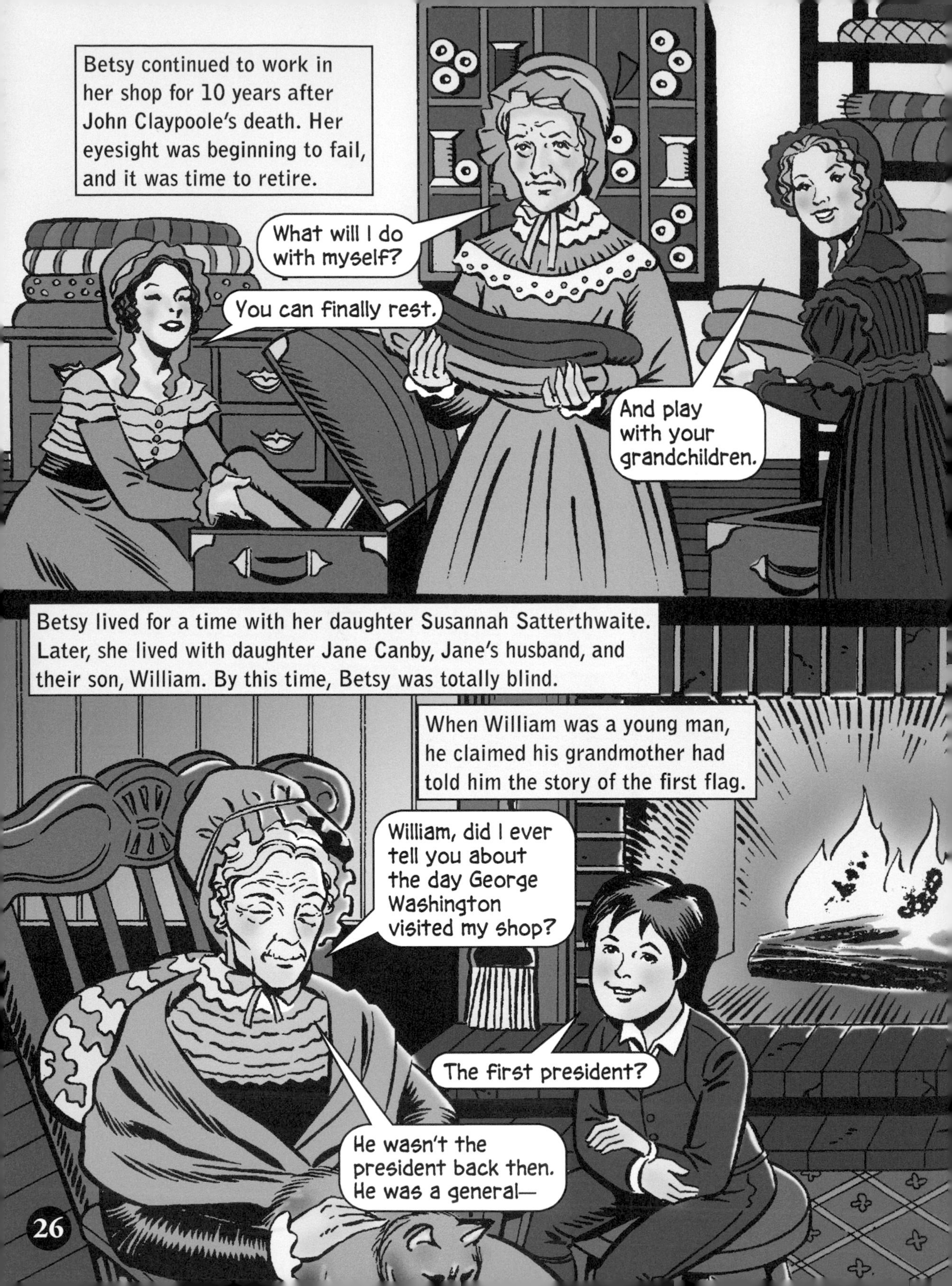
Betsy continued to work in her shop for 10 years after John Claypoole's death. Her eyesight was beginning to fail, and it was time to retire.
What will I do with myself?
You can finally rest.
And play with your grandchildren.
Betsy lived for a time with her daughter Susannah Satterthwaite. Later, she lived with daughter Jane Canby, Jane's husband, and their son, William. By this time, Betsy was totally blind.
When William was a young man, he claimed his grandmother had told him the story of the first flag.
William, did I ever tell you about the day George Washington visited my shop?
The first president?
He wasn't the president back then. He was a general—

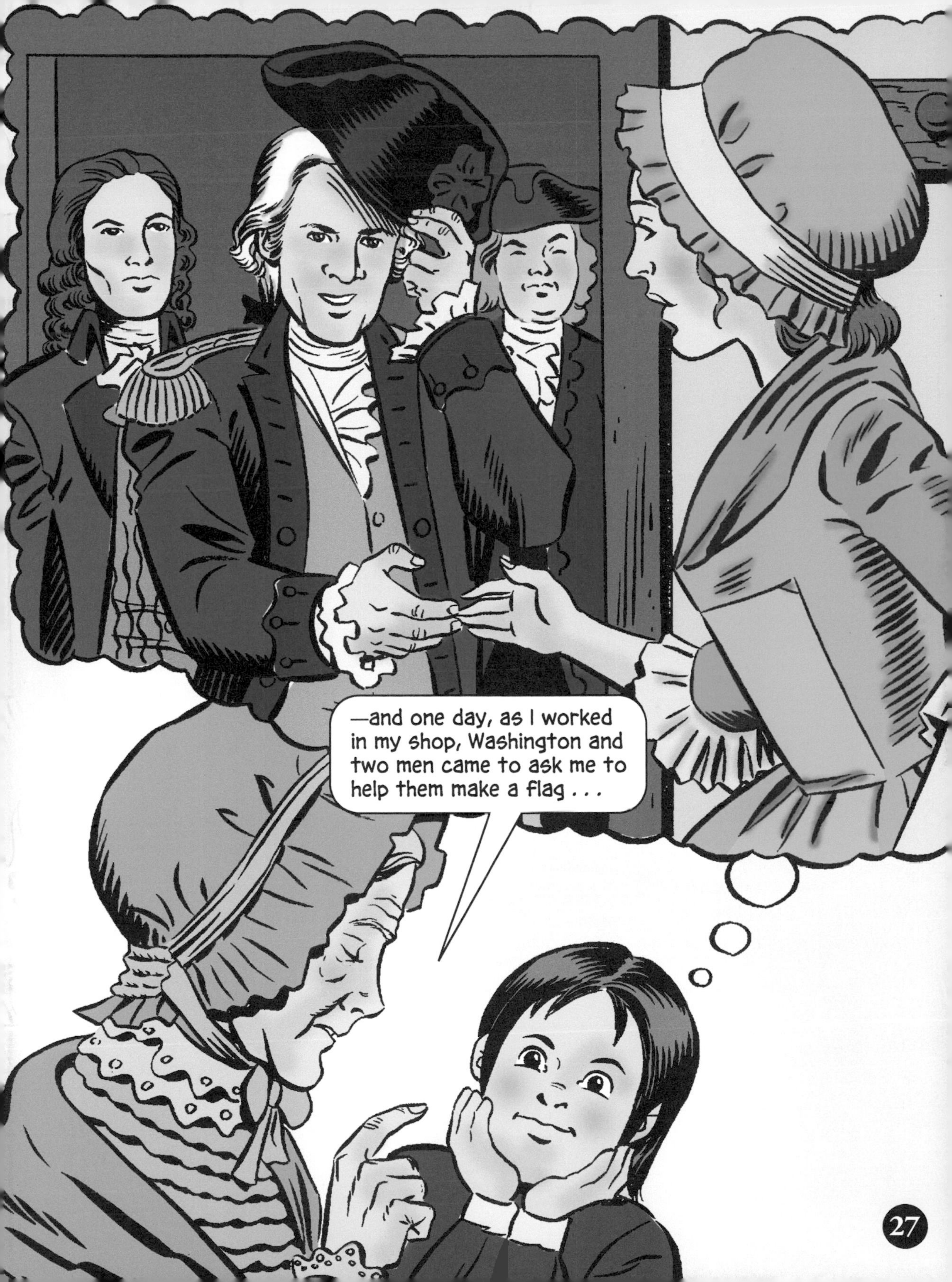
—and one day, as I worked in my shop, Washington and two men came to ask me to help them make a flag . . .

MORE ABOUT
BETSY ROSS
AND THE FLAG

★ Betsy Ross was born January 1, 1752. She died January 30, 1836. She was 84 years old.

★ In March 1870, Betsy's grandson, William Canby, told the Pennsylvania Historical Society the story of his grandmother making the first American flag. In July 1873, *Harper's Monthly* magazine published an article about Betsy Ross and the flag. Whether or not it is true, the legend of Betsy Ross began with this story.

★ Betsy had seven daughters. Lucilla, called Zillah, and Elizabeth, called Eliza, were daughters of Joseph Ashburn. Clarissa Sidney, Susannah, Rachel, Jane, and Harriet were daughters of John Claypoole. Lucilla died when she was a few years old. Harriet died before her first birthday.

★ Betsy has been buried in three different locations. The first was Christ Church Cemetery, followed by Mount Moriah Cemetery in Philadelphia. She now rests in a grave on Arch Street in the courtyard next to the Betsy Ross House in Philadelphia.

★ ## Reasons People Doubt the Legend of the Flag

There is no written record of anyone sewing the first American flag. George Washington wrote nothing about it in his letters or in his diary. No bill of sale or receipt exists to show Betsy sewed for Washington.

William Canby was 11 years old when Betsy Ross died. He did not tell his grandmother's story until almost 30 years later. He may have forgotten important details or made up some of the story.

In 1780, Francis Hopkinson sent a bill to the United States government. He wanted to be paid for the "design of the flag of the United States of America."

Congress shows no records of a flag committee. No one can prove that George Washington, Robert Morris, or George Ross ever asked anyone to sew the first American flag.

★ Reasons Some People Believe the Legend of the Flag

Francis Hopkinson was never paid for his claim to have designed the first American flag. In fact, many people believe that what he designed was a Naval flag and not the stars and stripes.

Samuel Wetherill was a friend of Betsy Ross. He told his family he visited Betsy shortly after she met with Washington, Morris, and Ross. Wetherill asked Betsy if he could keep the five-pointed paper star she had cut. In 1925, the Wetherills opened an old family safe. Inside was a paper star.

GLOSSARY

ammunition (am-yuh-NISH-uhn)—things that can be fired from weapons

apprentice (uh-PREN-tiss)—someone who learns a trade or craft by working with a skilled person

elope (ee-LOPE)—to run away and get married without others knowing about it

legend (LEJ-uhnd)—a story handed down from earlier times; most legends probably are not true.

Patriot (PAY-tree-uht)—a person who sided with the colonies during the Revolutionary War

Quaker (KWAY-kur)—a member of the religious group known as the Society of Friends

tax (TAKS)—the money collected from a country's citizens to help pay for running a government

upholstery (uhp-HOHL-stur-ee)—the fabric used to make furniture coverings

INTERNET SITES

FactHound offers a safe, fun way to find Internet sites related to this book. All of the sites on FactHound have been researched by our staff.

Here's how:

1. *Visit www.facthound.com*
2. Type in this special code **0736849629** for age-appropriate sites. Or enter a search word related to this book for a more general search.
3. Click on the **Fetch It** button.

FactHound will fetch the best sites for you!

READ MORE

Armentrout, David and Patricia. *Betsy Ross.* Discover the Life of an American Legend. Vero Beach, Fla.: Rourke, 2004.

Devillier, Christy. *Betsy Ross.* A Buddy Book. Edina, Minn.: Abdo, 2004.

Duden, Jane. *Betsy Ross.* Let Freedom Ring. Mankato, Minn.: Bridgestone Books, 2002.

Franchino, Vicky. *Betsy Ross: Patriot.* Our People. Chanhassen, Minn.: Child's World, 2003.

BIBLIOGRAPHY

The Betsy Ross House
http://www.betsyrosshouse.org/

The Legend of Betsy Ross
http://www.usflag.org/history/aboutbetsyross.html

Morris, Robert. *The Truth about the Betsy Ross Story.* Beach Haven, N.J.: Wynnehaven Publishing Co., 1982.

Parry, Edwin S. *Betsy Ross: Quaker Rebel.* Chicago: The John C. Winston Co., 1930.

INDEX